AF538852

G.B. Shaw's Drama

Unfolding Revolutionary Concept of Evolution

Mehar Fatima

PUBLISHERS & DISTRIBUTORS (P) LTD

Published by

PUBLISHERS & DISTRIBUTORS (P) LTD

7/22, Ansari Road, Darya Ganj, New Delhi-110002
Phones : +91-11-40775252, 23273880, 23275880, 23280451
Fax: +91-11-23285873
Web: www.atlanticbooks.com
E-mail: orders@atlanticbooks.com

Branch Office
5, Nallathambi Street, Wallajah Road, Chennai-600002
Phones : +91-44-48531784, 28411383
E-mail: chennai@atlanticbooks.com

Printed in India at Nice Printing Press, A-33/3A, Site-IV,
Industrial Area, Sahibabad, Ghaziabad, U.P.

Dedicated to

The venerable memory of
Hazrat Syed Shah Amanullah Quadri Mujeebi
(May Allah's choicest blessings be upon him!)
my spiritual mentor, who introduced me to the first lesson in Allama bil-Qalam
(the use of pen).

Foreword

This book lucidly serves to accommodate and comprehensively interprets G.B. Shaw's philosophy and art in the light of his drama. Every great art has some set goals to achieve and some mission to accomplish. According to G.B. Shaw, his mission is to "convert people to my opinion." To some of his readers the tone of his declaration may sound rather, imperious and most often unconventional. Yet, we can hardly dispute the assertion, since what he aspires to achieve is quite in line with the purity and strength of his mission, so much traceable with variations of form and expression in every great piece of art and literature through the ages. For instance, Shaw's Life force serving Creative Evolution can be found to carry as much fire and force of assertion as Alfred Tennyson's affirmation:

> And God fulfils Himself in many ways,
> Lest one good custom should corrupt the world.

Or, P. B. Shelly's aspiration to acquire the unbridled influence, along with the marvelous concealed spirit of service for reform and transformation as rendered by the "Wild West Wind" through its dynamic "unseen presence."

Truly enough, behind the artist, the dramatist, the poet, or whatever goes in the name of art and literature, stands the thinker, the visionary and the message giver, first in the shape of a rebel and secondly, a revolutionary to execute his reform.

As rightly pointed out by the author of this book, Shaw's revolt or rebellion is an open declared war waged against century old social, moral, economic and political institutions and their ills around the world. But Shaw, the revolutionary keeps his cool; he never loses sight of the reform and the deliverer within.

His art of drama is remarkably sustained and nourished by the divine inspiration gushing forth from, as has been referred to by the author, as Life Force which is the protector as well as executioner of Dr. Iqbal's "Divine Trust," in the sharp context of Shaw's own Creative Evolution.

It is for the reader to consider how far this book has been able to interpret Shaw's philosophy, art, and his mission.

Syed Sami Ahmed Quadri Mujeebi

Preface

Perceived along the natural continuity of life, with breaks and boons, yet centering round the search for vision and insight, this book led me through such an exploration of reality and miracles, imagination and consciousness, all convincing that learning is a long long process. Based on research, the book, *G.B. Shaw's Drama: Unfolding Revolutionary Concept of Evolution* has been so intensely part of my being, both inner and outer, that I would like to call it my first creation.

My interest in G.B. Shaw sprang from the power and strength of what is called idea, perhaps much before entering my research arena. My father's profound teaching in our (sisters and brothers) early days was adapting our eyes and minds to intense mystical, philosophical, literary, and scholarly discussions. And Shaw has always been a much discussed man at home. Papa instilled in me an enormous interest in literature, so much that my early home readings of Shavian plays like *Candida*, *Arms and the Man*, *Pygmalion*, and *Man and Superman* ignited passionate excitement of learning that often left me looking for more. I knew there was much more than mere drama in these plays. Years later, this curiosity recurred to me when we started sorting out a topic for my research through ideas, theories, and eras. A huge canvas, a lot of time, perennial ink, and an enthusiastic mind were needed to paint the ever-progressing picture of life.

Now, something of what I understand of Shaw. As we know, every true or great art provides inspiration and message powerful enough to solve issues pertaining to human institutions. What benefit does an art provide if not these? Shaw's drama is a judicious and creative effort of what he wants to say. And he says what he thinks. What worried him was not only that "The Garden of Eden", a symbol of life, was getting covered with weeds but that somebody from thinking masses should weed it properly. Amazing thoughts, intentions and actions make George Bernard Shaw one of the wonders of world literature. He would like to explore new ideas, but it is not enough that his choice is for new ideas; it is primarily because of his critical bend and sharpness of observation that he likes to see them in new moulds, and change them for the better. His search is for rectification of past mistakes, so as to build new edifices on the ashes of the old, useless and dead, making him a rebel, and a revolutionary. Professor Henry Higgins, in Shaw's masterpiece, *Pygmalion*, is almost echoing the playwright's inner voice, stressing that man "...is a human being with a soul and the divine gift of articulate speech." You will find circumstances and reasons of where and why Shaw stands for improvement and enrichment of human personality, the final shape of which will be 'superman', centering on human personality and its prospects.

Shaw thinks deeply and effectively over life and the creation of the earth and the heavens, and finds the whole divine system in the grip of evolution with its great promises for man and society. It is indeed a matter of tremendous courage that he makes us face the challenges, spelling tests and trials. So, the whole creation and the drama of life have some meaning, too real and challenging to be ignored. Shaw accepts these challenges and tries to see human life and its institutions within the working of time and space, keeping in mind the force and serviceability of history. It is in this context that he strongly recommends that art should be didactic and serviceable to life. Art for him is not perhaps, or should not be, a fairy tale or "fairy nothing", albeit artist's tall claims. Shaw's view of art is remarkably close to the realities of life but makes it subservient to ideals, like the breeze breathing fresh life into fruits and flowers—the "Westerly Wind" serving reorientation of the elements, or like the dew drop producing the pearl. Apparently, in his drama, Shaw is seen working miracles, yet his concern is not making miracles but to grapple with the hard realities of life in the shape of the variety of institutions, whose rectifications and reconstruction he deems necessary. Like John Milton, Shaw would like to work according to the aim and purpose of the supreme creator. The germ of this revolution lies in Shaw's firm faith in creating out of the 'will', which is the product of 'desire' and by no means he is going to recommend regaining of the lost paradise in charity, but through the power of will, sincerity, and ceaseless effort. It is significant to note here, with reference to Shaw's creative passion for reform, in line with social, political, economic, and so on, that his attention towards English language received some modifications as he liked it to be. His punctuation diversions, dropping the final e, are some of the many examples you will encounter in his quoted lines.

I call my readers from both academic and non academic worlds with new consciousness to engage themselves in serious speculation, and ponder over the discussed issues.

Mehar Fatima

Acknowledgements

I thank my sustainer, the most beneficent and the most merciful Almighty Allah, through His Mercy for the universe, our beloved Prophet Mohammad (PBUH), for bestowing me with plenty. I pay obeisance to my spiritual leader Hazrat Syed Shah Aaitullah Quadri Mujeebi for his benign supplications.

I would like to recognize my indebtedness to my professor, Dr. Ila Sinha, Patna University, for her profound scholarly guidance. My allegiance is due to all my teachers for their continued enlightenment and support. I mention with gratitude the encouragements of Prof. (Dr.) S. Zahoor Qasim, former Vice Chancellor, Jamia Millia Islamia, Late Prof. (Dr.) S. Wahab Ashrafi, Prof. Sati Prashad, Prof. S. Imtiyaz Hasnain, Dr. Rizwan Khan and Dr. Rahmat Jahan. I thank my colleagues, and particularly Dr. Saba Basheer, for extending her valuable suggestions regarding publication of this book. I appreciate the inspiring role of my enthusiastic students. My bosom friends, Nudrat, Dr. Elham, Dr. Halah, and Suma, have been an eternal source of support. The constant encouragements of all my friends have truly been a leading force. I am also thankful to Zoya for her loving concern.

My mother, Mrs. Naz Fatima has been invariably the source and initials of my life and strength. Her grace, motivation, and supplications are with this book. Prof. (Dr.) S. Sami Ahmed, my father, my guru, a philosopher, and a wonderful friend, has been teaching me all I know and need to know. Under his invaluable mentorship, I learned to critically observe the mystery that cloaks reality in appearances. In the course of preparing the book, our infinite discussions helped to rediscover my being, creating ample space and possibility for retrospection. I own immeasurable gratitude to my husband, Dr. Raihan, for providing me with the desired academic habitat. I could not have been able to walk along this path and complete this book without his active involvement, patience, and unending support.

I acknowledge my obligations to my mother-in-law, Mrs. Sarwat and father-in-law Prof. (Dr.) Shakeel Ahmad, for taking sincere interest and offering consistent cooperation in my study. My respect is due to my loving aunt, Mrs. Maliha Muslim, for her concern in my academic endeavours. I received appropriate modifications for the book so kindly extended by my uncles Prof. (Dr.) S. Shameem Ahmed, Dr. S. Waseem Ahmed, Prof. S. Aziz Ahmed and Dr. S. Riyaz Ahmed.

I appreciate the loving attention and concern of my brothers and their wives, S. Afaque Ahmed and Sumaiya, S. Ashfaque Ahmed and Kahkashan. My deep recognition is due to my most loving sisters for their sustained moral involvement and their companionship; Dr. Saequa, for proving continued assistance and materials, combined efforts of Nigar and her husband Fahad for their help and motivations, and my adorable sister, Khadija, for painstakingly typing the script. This book brought us together very often, to spend memorable time which is now a nostalgic storehouse for fantastic moments of joy, allowing us to share the inspiration.

Last but not the least, I express my gratefulness to Atlantic Publishers & Distributers (P) Ltd. for the interest evinced in publishing this book.

Mehar Fatima

Contents

Chapter 1

Introduction

Human life by nature is nurtured and sustained upon the seeds of growth and expansion, so that no one particular stage in the journey of life can be said to be static or the be all and the end all. The process of growth and development, in fact, never stops; it flows on to complete the ever promising and dynamic attainment of evolution. The spirit behind this evolution however, is one of struggle and ceaseless efforts. The stresses and storms, odds and ends in the way of this journey of life, motivate rather than impede or obstruct the miraculous flow of life and its consequent understanding and interpretation through art and philosophy.

George Bernard Shaw, the one who champion the Creative Evolution in the realm of dramatic art, was born in Dublin in 1856; in a family of small Irish landowners. His father was a small landowner who eventually became a grain merchant, and his mother, though daughter of a country gentleman lived largely on music, being an opera singer. Shaw, the boy was ordinarily educated yet he had the curiosity to know the pros and cons of life which made him frequent the Irish National Gallery in pursuit of knowledge of the art of great composers. This urge to know and learn turned him analytical and creative, following his own later theory of desire, will and then creation, leading to seek his own way which gave him a discerning analytical and judicious view of art and life. Creation, as said earlier is said to be the result of continuous effort and struggle. On the other hand, for the one, short of insight and inner creative urge, the lack of material facilities and pleasures of life become clear obstructions on the way to progress. The early days of every genius have been one of struggles which ultimately lead him to construction and service. Shaw's early days, which in his own words were "rich only in dreams," is indicative enough of his tremendous future, his later creative capability and output. Thus curiosity and struggle gave him deep insight into human nature as well as the existing social and moral institutions. This curiosity to know and reform led him to try his hands at social novels which involved accurate observation and impartial analysis of society and the people, and finally paved his way to drama writing and the theatre. His concept and portrayals of characters in his novels, written between the years 1870-82, namely *Immaturity*, *The Irrational Knot*, and *Love Among the Artists*, provided him clues for his brilliant portrayals of characters in his Drama of Ideas and Purpose, which he later fully exploited to the point of emphasizing his philosophy of 'Life Force' and the concept of 'Superman'. Whether Shaw would have succeeded better or worse as a novelist is difficult to say, but one thing is certain that Shaw perhaps could succeed in anticipating the themes and ideas he was to exploit later in his drama. In order to have the right concept and growth of a writer's philosophy and his attitude towards life and social institutions, we cannot but look into the context in which his ideas and expressions picked up growth and expansion. What actually is the problem is that in the case of most of the philosophies and ideas of artists we fail to trace the background and context which could really be helpful in appreciating the evolutionary trends of the artist's genius. Shaw's novels incidentally fall in the years of his struggle, which led him to come across fresh personalities and brilliant visions. Contemporary writers and thinkers of repute such as Henry George, whose thought and revolutionary speeches, according to Shaw, "changed the whole current of my life", motivated Shaw towards socialism and the study of economics. Karl Marx's *Das Capital* also came under his serious attention and study. A host of other leading socialists and progressive idealists who influenced him were, Edward Carpenter, William Morris, and Sidney Web. Shaw's membership of the Fabian Society of London in 1885 became the climax of his involvement in serving to extend and flourish his deep involvement in socialism, through his developed attitude for debate and discussion from public speaking platforms and street corners. Evidently, all these helped to push Shaw towards exploring some dynamic means of art and expression, shaping him into a pioneering force in the theatre of Ideas and coordinating him to the great evolutionary trend which began with Robertson, William Archer, Arthur Pinero and Henrik Ibsen.

What Shaw actually did or was doing all these years, was like that of the bird, which, while it chirps and twitters on the boughs, keeps collecting materials to build its nest. Shaw was busy speaking and listening, exchanging views, discovering new ideas and thereby exploring ways and means to find a suitable artistic vehicle to carry forward the revolutionary strains of his ideas. Every creative effort in fact hinges on exploring new avenues like the honey bees' toiling to explore, collect and then ultimately serve. Shaw's careful and sharp insight into socialistic lessons, coupled with his unique philosophic bend lent him vision of a new better world, supported by his dedicated feelings for humanity at large. The socialism, that Shaw so far undertook to carry, lacked religious base which he was lucky enough to soon compensate from the writings of Samuel Butler. This indeed gave him a lucky escape from Darwin's theory of evolution which was based on the theory of chance rather than the concept of plan, possibility and hope. The idea of a purposive Life Force which was to throw up Shaw as the great creative thinker and dramatist of his times, puts him on the highly creative and intelligent handling of human endeavours towards the evolution of man to an improved social, moral, intellectual and economic level. The move and intention to discern, criticize and educate society may have been due to the happy combination of experience and coincidence, in the case of Shaw as some critics allege. Nevertheless it was perhaps more of what Shaw called "first desire", "then will" and finally "create" than the result of mere "chance" or "coincidence". His love of debate and discussion with the character's dual task of being both proposer and opposer, made the area of drama his very own province. Now with the arrival of his 'Plays Pleasant and Unpleasant' in 1898, Shaw shook the literary world with the announcement that a new brilliant star had appeared on the dramatic horizon who will soon strip the people and society of their social and moral complacencies. The new drama was now going to shatter the contemporary, social, political, economic, intellectual and religious trends of the time, with the dramatist as a unique and brilliant combination of the artist and the preacher.

No art or literature can grow without the background of its origin. In order to appreciate the development of Shaw's dramatic art, it is therefore, only imperative to trace the dramatic trends of nineteenth and twentieth centuries of literary drama in which, actually speaking, the theatre was decidedly on the decline especially after Sheridan and Goldsmith until the time of Victorian patronage, although there were attempts to revive the strings of Shakespeare's poetic dramatic style. Thus, melodrama and the farce had become the need of the hour which provided relief and entertainment from the high classical and serious drama, but slowly and gradually the needs and aspirations changed according to variation in changing times. It was later that the dramatists began to take inspiration from contemporary novels and fictions of Scott and Dickens. So as time passed, social values, crimes, war and rebellion entered the drama of the time, bringing domestic melodrama close to hard realities of life with various problems and issues that later on was to assume the status of new type of drama for a period from 1890-1920. The first in the series was Tom Robertson's *Society* (1865) and other plays under the name of domestic drama with excellent dramatic energy and theatrical sense. Then we have the distinguished name of Sir Arthur Pinero, a master of dramatic craft whose plays in spite of some sentimentalism and conventional treatment of characters, established him as the real pioneer of the twentieth-century realistic theatre, whose rich legacies of realistic dialogues and 'theatrical excitement' was later to be taken up by G.B. Shaw himself. In Shaw's hands this legacy of realistic drama further expanded into tremendous Plays of Ideas and Purpose. Shaw a super creative artist inspired by Henrik Ibsen, the Norwegian thinker-dramatist and fired by his own fresh new zeal and versatility of his genius and art, obsessed with his keen observation and brilliant analysis, gave new directions towards tracing contemporary social and moral diagnosis providing them with solutions. Eventually, the prose realistic drama got definite and surer roots under the name of Problem Plays. Shaw with his creative and innovative realistic problem plays, in fact, helped evolve the old melodrama and all the previous dramatic trends into a dynamic vehicle of social reflection and reform. He opened his dramatic account with his first revolutionary play *Widower's Houses*, questioning the established social norms and the existing social institutions which became the central theme and philosophy of his dramatic art in all his later plays. In this journey of the evolution of his dramatic art and philosophy of life, Shaw evidently followed the example of Henrik Ibsen, the celebrated Norwegian playwright only "to get away from idolatry and to get the truth regardless of shattered ideals."[1] Standing between two dramatic eras, as we may perceive, the Victorian and the Modern, Shaw in fact had the advantage of analyzing and evaluating the various trends of the art of the two periods, and like Ibsen holding discussion and interpretation rather than pursuing action or traditional unraveling of dramatic situation. Such challenging trends in the art of drama were bound to shock the critics, which evidently provoked them to the point of opposing this new dramatic setup of debate, discussion and explanation as only undramatic. To this Shaw through his preface in *Man and Superman,* retorted, "what I call drama is nothing but explanation."[2] In this way Shaw adapted the old ideas and trends to his own dramatic art with the objective to deal with real situations of life and society in pursuit of the causes behind the problems.

Idealism for Shaw is as damaging and obstructive to progress as sentimentalism or romanticism. Since personal righteousness and idealism are against Shaw's social realism and his concept of truth because like Ibsen's assertion of truth, which according to him, is 'in constant flux' and cannot be applied upon life by addressing a certain fixed rule. By his objectives therefore, Shaw as a realist justifies his stance against shallow sentimentalism because it is superficial, superstitious and blind to facts of life and can hardly comprehend real life situations. In fact, social and moral realities take place in the background of human nature and fortunately, Shaw's realistic analysis and attitude and his suitable dramatic technique could work. His plays like *Candida*, *The Devil's Disciple*, and *Arms and the Man*, and others can be said to be representative of such applications. Tracing Shaw's evolutionary trend in matter of thought, attitude and behaviour is part of understanding human life and nature. Shaw does accept liberty as a prestigious human attainment but he thinks, it can never be attained without undertaking a sense of responsibility to balance it. This sense of responsibility plays its basic role in any human progress or development whatsoever and also leads to brotherhood. An author of a Drama of Idea and Purpose, like Shaw, is supposed to have a searching eye for the causes behind human ignorance and anarchy.

Going through G.B. Shaw's plays, one is sure to have a feeling of acquainting with a great observer of real life situations. Shaw is a satirist with the intention of revolutionizing and reforming things around, yet remarkably maintaining the spontaneous sense of unity and coherence in the art of Drama of Ideas and Purpose. Beginning with the *Widower's Houses*, through *Man and Superman*, *Back to Methuselah*, and *Saint Joan*, all prove to be the brilliant illustrations of drama of evolution of both art and ideas. As for Shaw's application of revolutionary attitude in the art and ideas, *Saint Joan* is held as his masterpiece. Such plays like *Saint Joan* and other historical pieces, in fact, carry a revolutionary passion on the part of the artist. They connect the past, present and future, which we collectively call history. They have a continuity of human experience that coordinates the different historical periods, because human nature never changes. One of the relevant features of Shaw's evolutionary and progressive attitudes is his love and appreciation of historical subjects like the medieval art, culture and the medieval period itself. Close to William Morris and Ruskin and unlike Macaulay, Shaw argues that the superiority of Middle Ages is because of the medieval world's superiority as a society, and at the same time, the fall of religious art through sixteenth and nineteenth century was perhaps due to the eclipse of religion by the emerging science and commerce. Shaw's Life Force, upon which, he structured his most dynamic philosophy of life, interestingly enough comes in direct clash with Darwin's theory of Natural Selection, which unlike Shaw's "purposeful design" bases itself upon pure chance and accident. It is, in fact, the sum total of our dramatist's main focus on the concept and theory of life that relates itself to the spiritual and divine base of creation, coupled with the tremendous legacy of the "divine trust" to the future generation. Over and above, for Shaw, the fundamental significance is what the writer has to say. This clearly refers to the Drama of Idea and Purpose, the burden of which Shaw undertook upon his shoulders and carried forward to the next set of artists and future dramatists. Truly enough, Shaw is nothing if not a message giver, the one who is all the time reminding us with the words already echoing in his reader's ears, "But 'for art's sake' alone I would not face the toil of writing a single sentence."[3] Deeply integrated to this message giving is the concept of Problem Plays and Play of Ideas through his remarkable prefaces because they not only supplement the plays but provide force and strength to his ideas and the style of his assertion. Side by side with his wonderful employment of prefaces, his dramatic devices and techniques like wit and humour and the unique use of paradoxes, can hardly be overlooked. The significant point here is that all such devices and employment of Shaw's techniques tend to help and carry forward the intended message or rather become part of the message and the idea itself. The subsequent chapters have much to discus in this regard. Nonetheless, this employment of wit and humour with the passage of time has made Shaw's drama pick up pace of evolution and maturity in his art and ideas attaining full ripening and therefore, giving stronger effect. This is evident especially when we study Shaw's masterpieces like *Man and Superman*, *Saint Joan*, and *Back to Methuselah*, which appear to declare a surer voice of the dramatist, his higher flight and employment of a wider range of thought and matter.

In order to move further, we must question firstly as to what is drama, what are to be its basic components and fundamentals? One has to define drama to settle the query, whether it is simply a story told or a plot enacted with a dramatic air, just to excite and entertain the readers and the playgoers, or is it a vehicle of attaining some higher objectives or some means of expression for conveying new ideas and purpose. The answers to all such baffling queries in fact, refer back to the concept of drama and the environment attributed to it. The making of the earth and the heavens out of nothing, the creation of mankind in the form of Adam and Eve, their coming down upon the earth, are all perhaps the beginning of what we may call drama or dramatic venture. The spirit of earth welcoming Adam and Eve so dramatically depicted by Dr. Iqbal, the noted poet and philosopher of the East, would be worth quoting here some lines from the piece, which so artfully captivates the dramatic element behind the 'Fall' and further serve to observe and interpret by explaining the scheme involving creation. It is the earth addressing Adam:

> Open thine eyes! Look at the earth, the air, the heavens,
> Look thou at the brilliant sun, rising from the east,
> Look at the Veiled Unveiled, concealed under the Veil,
> Look at the parting, its pangs, its agonies,
> Loose not thine heart, gear up thine hope, its fruition sweet,
> Wilt reach soon the Heavens thine tears, thine longings,
> Built thou thine self,
> Oh! Evolution is thine.[4]

History is evident that the creation of the earth and the heavens and the consequent creation of Man and Woman was the first and the foremost original source of all stories told across the world literature. It is now understandable that the drama or the dramatic story, if it has to appeal and stay or survive should be creative and evolutionary. We, therefore, can say that drama needs to have some important elements for its effect and appeal. First, in order to observe among these elements is the availability of a plot and a story powerful enough to engage the playgoers. Characters and characterization is another vital component along with its drammaticality of expression and suspense. Last, but not least, is the actor's skilful performance.

We can trace back the beginnings of English drama from the time succeeding the arrival of the Normans. The earliest reference to dramatic representation in England is the performance of a Latin play in honour of St. Catherine at about 1110 A.D. By the time of the Norman Conquest, religion and evolution of the rich symbolic liturgy of the church seems to have established itself in France, ultimately finding its entry into England. Their aim was simply didactic, which was meant to instruct the unlettered masses in the truth of their religion. In the very beginning, this drama remained under complete control of the church. Performances were always given in the sacred buildings and the actors were the priest, with the Latin at their service being the language employed. They began to be called 'mystery' and 'miracle' plays and grew in acceptance of public popularity with religious emphasis, to the extent that these plays travelled "from the porch into the churchyard and from the precincts of the church altogether to the village green or the city street,"[5] with the vernacular tongue, first French then English having been substituted for the original Latin. However, the religious drama in England could not reach its zenith until the fourteenth century, depicting the highly captivating tale of the Creation of the World and the Fall of man with such prophetic themes as the Flood, the sacrifice of Isaac, and the Crucifixion, Resurrection, and Ascension, closing with the Last Judgment. Though crude in literary quality, these stories touched the note of pathos and the chord of tragedy. A remarkable point here is that at this point there was introduction of comic element as in the Shepherd plays of the Wakefield series, which is deeply reflective of the growth of the dramatic sense.

The fact is that this sort of drama evolved into 'morality' play. Although very much like the 'miracle' play with a didactic touch, the characters were personified abstractions like Signs, Perseverance, Free Will, and Seven Deadly Sins, in place of belonging to sacred narrative or legends of the saints. The rise of this form of drama naturally coincided with the proper allegorical poetry of the time. A later product of the dramatic development of the morality play is what is known as Interlude, specifically signifying a short dramatic piece of satire rather than of a directly religious or an ethical strain. Viewing historically, these experiments in drama were simply brilliant and epoch making, producing a kind of 'Dames School' for English dramatic genius and eventually did a lot towards paving ground for regular drama. The renaissance and its eventual impact with its revival of learning dominated these preliminary phases of dramatic development into popular and established art, compelling people to go back to the classics for inspiration, falling back upon the models more of Latin than of Greek playwrights. The evolution of dramatic art in the form of comedy and tragedy in this way continued until it reached academic circles like universities and scholarly audiences and men of letters. This was followed by Latin imitation paving the way for attempts to fashion English plays upon the patterns of the originals. Needless to say that many valuable lessons in the principles of dramatic construction and technique were brought home to the English dramatists, producing the first English comedy named *Roister Doister* by Nicolas Udall in 1550. At the very same time Gorboduc became the first real tragedy based on the form and spirit of Senacan tragedy. It is noteworthy that technically and aesthetically Gorboduc will go down in history of drama as the first English tragedy to have Blank verse, which historically was to become a remarkable tool in the hands of our dramatic legend, the great poet dramatist, William Shakespeare, which most suited the needs of the romantic air of Shakespeare's drama. It was also the cherished dream of George Bernard Shaw, who wished to write in Blank verse. We find him saying, "I am fond of Blank verse."[6]

However, the introduction and consequent popularity of *Gorboduc* produced a sort of clash and conflict between the classic dramas which followed the Italian Senacian style. Its form and model and the pressing Romantic taste had inclination of the British Theatre taste which resulted in the final triumph and establishment of the Romantic drama. In fact, this triumph of the Romantic mode of drama owes itself to Shakespeare's immediate predecessors; a group of brilliant galaxy of scholars and dramatists remembered as University Wits.

Profiting by the classical concept and dramatic techniques, these extraordinary trained scholars and craftsmen succumbed to the free tradition of the popular stage. The legacy of it was to be taken up and enriched by William Shakespeare in the form of romantic drama, which later was to undergo a tremendous transformation in the hands of G.B. Shaw as the Drama of Ideas and Purpose. The process of evolution in art and literature is said to be not so simple, it is no smooth sail. The path is shown with ups and downs and there is no dearth of bumps or jerks with many shocking turns. This is evident when we talk of Ben Jonson, who being the most unavoidable and closest of Shakespeare's immediate contemporaries, deviated from the main contemporary romantic trend, taking to Drama of Manners. Now, a little later in early seventeenth century, we travel up to the times of Comedy of Restoration, where we come across two most important dramatists, William Wycherley (1640-1716) and William Congreve (1670-1729). This Comedy of Manners will remain historically significant in a particular context that nearly a century later G.B. Shaw did something miraculous out of it. He carved his own Comedy of Purpose out of the resemblance of what Congreve and Wycherley gave to the British drama called Comedy of Manners. It can be observed in the course of this book that without this base, Shavian drama would have left an important genre untouched.

Nevertheless, when Shaw looked at the British theatre of his times, he seemed to have had cried 'Look around you' echoing Christopher Wren's anxious call to the Londoners when the city was afire. It remains a fact that the British theatre at the beginning of Shaw's career when he arrived in the city, was in shambles. With the power and style of his forceful prose drama, and all his brilliant wit and humour, and paradoxes, he took the plot of his drama out of the four walls of the theatre, giving it a realistic and problem solving touch.

Shaw's dramatic genius with his unerring and penetrating eye on the infirmities of the contemporary institutions, and his rare analytical acumen, transformed the entire world of drama in England into problem solving institution and a centre of reform. It was way back in 1876 that Shaw travelled up to London from Dublin in the almost penniless condition and made politics and journalism a springboard to public notice and personality recognition. He became a regular Hyde Park speaker which thrived on interesting and fiery speeches against the administration as well as social institutions. All this prepared him for a new type of drama; the Drama of Ideas supported by his amazing inborn wit and humour. In preface to *The Devil's Disciple* he admits:

> I first caught the ear of the British public on a cart in Hyde Park, to the blaring of brass bands, and this not at all as a reluctant sacrifice of my instinct of privacy to political necessity, but because, like all dramatists and mimes of genuine vocation, I am a natural-born mountebank.[7]

No wonder, Shaw's satirical but creative analysis of the contemporary social, moral, and political situations of the time helped sharpen his tools for management and handling of the theatre and dramatic techniques. So the theatre for him became instrumental for exposition of moral passion for reform and social relationship covering religion, finance, prostitution, even housing, and domestic conditions. In short nothing could escape his eagle eyes. What made Shaw evolve from a propagandist to a playwright, a thinker and a philosopher is his dealing with real life problems of men and women of blood and bones, a genuine and deep reflection upon human life, its nature, and his passion for moral reform. This evolution from a propagandist to a playwright appears to have taken place perhaps between *Widower's Houses*, *Candida* and *You Never Can Tell*. However, the best was yet to come. It was *Man and Superman* that offered, the tremendous and fresh idea of his theory of Life Force, which according to Shaw was the guiding force to instil into man the higher purpose of life to produce and accomplish human personality in the form of superman who would be "God's coadjutor on earth."[8]

Our point of study here is that the most significant aspect in building up of drama is the creative urge and the supremacy of idea and philosophy which the dramatist is obliged to possess, in order to coordinate with the practical human life. We have the legendary figures that excelled in the art of drama like Shakespeare and Marlowe in England, the celebrated German Goethe, the Italian Dante, Kalidasa of ancient India and Tagore of modern India. Drama in the hands of these artists had the story of Adam and Eve retold and, thus, with variations of it in changing times, we develop a special artistic sense to see and feel it. For sure drama is part of the life of man, the print of which is writ large on the sands of time. For instance, Shakespeare's celebrated line:

> Tomorrow and tomorrow and tomorrow creeps in this petty pace from day to day.
>
> ...it's a tale told by an idiot, full of sound and fury,
>
> Signifying nothing.[9]

Macbeth's tragic experience of extreme frustration and anguish is beautifully portrayed, which has its own interest and striking dramatic elements. Thus, we see that the creative urge for dramatic expression implicit in the very life of man is hard to be disputed. Or we can take Christopher Marlowe's famous lines from *Doctor Faustus*, signifying man's demon appetite to acquire more and more:

> Go forward, Faustus, in that famous art wherein all natures treasure is contained. Be thou on earth as Jove is in the sky, Lord and commander of these elements.[10]

A single line would be enough to show Kalidasa's dramatic presentation from *Abhijhnana Sakuntalam*, "where shall a great river bend its course if not to the sea."[11] It signifies the course of nature so eventually that the art of drama like the art of poetry and music thrives on one base of evolution, whether it is the poetic dramatic excellence of Shakespeare or the prose dramatic genius of Shaw. The pioneering force every time, we can see, is nothing but evolution. The art of drama is impregnated with the spirit of life, deeply rooted into the ground and is budding forth with the sense of commitment and service to mankind. It is indeed, a point of reflection and research to understand the creative urge of the dramatist which makes the art of drama evolutionary. This creative urge behind the evolution, through the stresses and strains of time pacing with the slow and steady toil of centuries, seems to have eventually assumed the status of what we call Drama of Idea and Purpose. Shaw through his Caesar declares in rhetorical style, "Is peace not an art? Is war not an art? Is government not an art? Is civilization not an art?"[12] Therefore his drama can be clearly seen capable of dealing with all the possible institutions of society in order to evolve them into higher destiny.

Indeed, the artist's honest handling with perception and insight makes all moves and actions artistic. The dramatist and his art, if not evolutionary and creative, are worth nothing. Its plot, characters and characterization, values and customs, as well as tradition concerning art will sound and look shallow and superficial without this urge to expand, evolve and enrich. The mind and pen of the dramatist has to be necessarily creative. Of course, it remains one of the pioneering attainments of creative evolution that provides key to the treasures of wisdom and learning, thus motivating enjoyment and understanding of the work of art and drama in particular and the multifarious widely spread institutions of life in general.

Shaw remains a tireless crusader for social justice and righteousness. He began as a propagandist for the intellectual enlightenment of the people in general, with zealous mission as a social reformer. Shaw's criticism on society may appear to be destructive, but if at all it is so, it breaks the chains which had held society in mental thrall. He is seen in his works trying to liberate his age from hypocritical ways, mental sloth, contemporary social ills, superstition, idealism, romanticism, and sentimentalism, and all the stagnant ideas which had not been consciously subjected to the tests of real life and honest thought. In Epistle dedicatory to Arthur Walkley, Shaw explains his art of dramatic writing. He writes, "I do not adulterate the product with aphrodisiacs nor dilute it with romance and water."[13] And he appreciates artists of the same kind. Martin Meisel in his Treatise, *Shaw and the Nineteenth Century Theatre* has focused on Shaw's realistic approach towards writers. He observed:

> The sharpest distinction Shaw ever made between writers was not between good and bad, though he deliberately chooses the term "writers of the first order" and "writers of the second order". A work of a writer of the first order is one in which the morality is original and not readymade.[14]

Shaw's sharp, brilliant, and deep insight into human character, situations and circumstances make him a distinguished dramatist. It is necessary for a serious artist and critic of life like Shaw to possess a highly imaginative mind along with broader outlook and wider universal sympathies. His works reflect his keen observation of both individual and society with minute details of day-to-day events. We can find his mastery and maturity over his expression and style in his prose dramatic domain. Rhythmic tones in his dialogues often so rhyme as to produce the desired effect of conveying his message. He acquired this from his mother, who happened to be an opera singer. However, his prose style seems to merge dramatically in respect of plot with the tools of wit and humour and paradoxes, providing variety and spice to his ideas. Yet, Shaw provides concrete truth in his works. This involves his attempt to critically study various aspects of social life, and its morals.

Shaw's plays aimed at altering the existing social, moral as well as economic orders like those of Henrik Ibsen's. But unlike Ibsen who left the problems unsolved, Shaw went ahead to provide suitable and apt solutions to them in his very own way. Ibsen had no ethical motive, while Shaw took up drama for revolution in society and its values. It is surprising to find Shaw dealing with didactic motivations into Ibsen's works in his *Quintessence of Ibsenism*. Michael Holroyod in the introduction to this book notes, "He (Shaw) is not concerned here with Ibsen as a poet and dramatist but as a teacher...."[15] The book also presents Shaw's credentials as someone who was carrying on Ibsen's business of "Changing the mind of Europe."[16] Shaw with a mission to transform the old face of society, tried to distil Ibsen's message to his own time. As a thinker and a committed artist, he continues to free contemporary society from its romantic delusions and outmoded conventions, refurnishing it with rational values and sound principles. Though serious in approach, one cannot fail to observe his comic sensibility, firmly rooted in an uncompromising rationalism. His comic genius and his sense of wit and humour are undeniable. It is in his prefaces that he sets to spell out his serious tone, his plays carry his philosophic ideas along with comic episodes and humorous events. These tactics are to involve the readers and the audiences, but it comes so naturally to Shaw as if it was intrinsic in the dramatist.

Shaw's characters are often mixed, they do not come in sets and so it is one of his observed principles of human character.

Louis Dubedat in *Doctor's Dilemma* is one of the notable examples of a moral scoundrel. To give mixed characters as one's heroes, Shaw's opinion is that it is dramatically necessary on the wide modern stage. The audiences of today demand a hero who:

> ...instead of walking, talking, eating, drinking, sleeping, making love, and fighting single combats in a monotonous ecstasy of continuous heroism, are heroic in the true human fashion: that is, touching the summits only at rare moments, and finding the proper level of all occasions, condescending with humour and good sense to the prosaic ones as well as rising to the noble ones, instead of ridiculously persisting in rising to them all on the principle that a hero must always soar, in season and out of season.[17]

The hero specifically here, in Shaw's mind is perhaps his Julius Caesar.

The concept of the Shavian Superman can be traced back to that of Nietzsche's. Nietzsche does not see any harm in the affliction and suffering of the common people, if it is indispensable for the fulfilment of the purpose of a great man. The reason for revolution for him is because, "the Revolution made Napoleon possible: that is its justification. We ought to desire the anarchical collapse of the whole of our civilization if such a reward were to be the result."[18] But for Shaw, the common mass is held responsible for breeding a great man. His Superman is free from the bonds of conventional morality. The 'Will' as Nietzsche conceives of it, seeks power as an end but Shaw recognizes it as one of the forms in which Life Force expresses itself. It is the conquest of the self; control of passions, by willpower that Shaw expresses these in a realistic fashion. His realism is obvious in C.E.M. Joad's remark:

> Shaw's realism falls into four categories; women, artists, men of action and of course the Irish...An Whitfield, the Millionaires', Candida, St. Joan are all examples of feminine realists. Louis Dukelat and Eugene Marchbanks speak for the artists, Caesar and Napoleon, among others, for the men of action.[19]

Realism for Shaw is based upon philosophy of real life and living people. But very often critics fail to accept or understand his viewpoint and philosophy. And, we thus have Shaw's response:

> As to the philosophy, I taught my critics the little they know in my *Quintessence of Ibsenism*; and now they turn their guns—the guns I loaded for them—on me, and proclaim that I write as if mankind had intellect without will, or heart, as they call it. Ingrates: who was it I that directed your attention to the distinction between Will and Intellect? Not Schopenhauer, I think, but Shaw.[20]

Shaw is very much aware of his dramatic stance and the purpose behind his motive, for he declares himself a responsible artist who worked to erase misconceptions showing proper distinctions between things. Perhaps his boldness stems from his revolutionary background. In the preface to *John Bull's Other Island*, Shaw traces his pedigree rather proudly. He writes:

> I am a genuine typical Irishman of the Danish, Norman, Cromwellian, and (of course) Scottish invasion. I am violently and arrogantly Protestant by family tradition.[21]

Shaw did not budge from his firm position, it is a fact that the creed which Shaw had been teaching in the very early part of his dramatic career, was continued with him in the last part of his life when he was in his nineties. We can trace him struggling to revolutionise the two ages, the Victorian and the Modern. In the last part of his life, he is reported to have said that he dreaded success, because to have succeeded is to have finished one's work or business on earth. He always liked his goals to be in front of him and not behind. Truly enough, he can be seen dominating the English theatre for over sixty years and his influence, name and fame are all pervasive even today. Most of the critics are unanimous that Shaw remains one of the greatest dramatic figures in the late nineteenth and early twentieth century drama. It only remains to say that, "our age needed a new Aquinas and we were given G.B. Shaw."[22]

Shaw's plays and his works mark a tremendously continued effort towards evolution and growth. He is essentially a philosopher with some higher message to impart. His appeal is universal, breaking down barriers of nations, caste, colour, and creed. His dreams and visions have potentials to come to reality, having the courage to face and respond to the emerging challenges. We should explore and substantiate ahead that Shaw is a confirmed optimist, he is forward looking, and his ideas have the capacity to move mountains and bring miraculous changes. In fact, his agenda is all embracing and comprehensive with the vision of creating the Superman. Thus, the idea and objective behind his concept of evolution in art, and drama in specific, is evidently a mark of a continued pulsating life, artfully equipped with meeting the perennial demands and challenges of the changing times and situations.

Notes

1. Shaw. "Introduction." *Major Critical Essays. England*, Middlesex: Penguin, 1986. p. 11.
2. Shaw. "Epistle Dedicatory." *Man and Superman*. ed. Dan H.L. *The Bodely Head Bernard Shaw Collected Plays with their Prefaces*. Vol. 2. London: Max Reinhardt, 1980. p. 494.
3. *Ibid*., p. 527.
4. Mohammad Iqbal. "Bale-Jibraeel." *Kulliyate-Iqbal*. Delhi: Kutub Khana Azizia, 2002. p. 351.
5. W.H. Hudson. *An Outline History of English Literature*. Delhi: A.I.T.B.S., 2007. p. 31.
6. Shaw. "Preface." *The Admirable Bashville*. ed. Dan H.L. *The Bodely Head Bernard Shaw Collected Plays with their Prefaces*. Vol. 2. London: Max Reinhardt, 1980. p. 433.
7. Shaw. "On Diabolonian Ethics." The Devil's Disciple. ed. Dan H.L. *The Bodely Head Bernard Shaw Collected Plays with their Prefaces*. Vol. 2. London: Max Reinhardt, 1980. pp. 29-30.
8. W.H. Hudson. *An Outline History of English Literature*. Delhi: A.I.T.B.S., 2007. p. 277.
9. William Shakespeare. *Macbeth*. Delhi: Rupa, 2003. p. 97.
10. Christopher Marlow. *Doctor Faustus*. United States: Kessinger. 2004. p. 100.
11. Kalidasa. *Abhijhnana Shakuntalam*. Delhi: Rama Brothers, 2006. p. 47.
12. Shaw. "Caesar and Cleopatra." Act V. ed. Dan H. L. *The Bodely Head Bernard Shaw Collected Plays with their Prefaces*. Vol. 2. London: Max Reinhardt, 1980. p. 288.

13. Shaw. "Epistle Dedicatory." *Man and Superman*. ed. Dan H.L. *The Bodely Head Bernard Shaw Collected Plays with their Prefaces*. Vol. 2. London: Max Reinhardt, 1980. pp. 503-04.
14. Martin Meisel. *Shaw and the Nineteenth Century Theatre*. New Jersey: Princeton University Press, 1963. p. 91.
15. Michael Holroyd. "Introduction." *Major Critical Essays*. Harmondsworth, Middlesex: Penguin, 1986. p. 46.
16. *Ibid.*
17. Shaw. "Bernard Shaw and the Heroic Actor." *Caesar and Cleopatra*. ed. Dan H.L. *The Bodely Head Bernard Shaw Collected Plays with their Prefaces*. Vol. 2. London: Max Reinhardt, 1980. p. 307.
18. Bertrand Russell. *History of Western Philosophy*. London: Unwin Brothers, 1954. p. 790.
19. C.E.M. Joad. *Shaw and Society*. London, 1953. p. 268.
20. Shaw. "On Diabolonian Ethics." *The Devil's Disciple*. ed. Dan H.L. *The Bodely Head Bernard Shaw Collected Plays with their Prefaces*. Vol. 2. London: Max Reinhardt, 1980. p. 29.
21. Shaw. "Preface for Politicians." *John Bull's Other Island*. ed. Dan H.L. *The Bodely Head Bernard Shaw Collected Plays with their Prefaces*. Vol. 2. London: Max Reinhardt, 1980. p. 811.
22. Ifor Evans. *A Short History of English Literature*. Harmondsworth: Penguin, 1961. p. 126.

Chapter 2

Development of Shaw's Dramatic Art

Having traced the right and the required concept and understanding of Shaw's dramatic genius, we can now proceed to find out how drama really evolved and developed in the hands of this great creative artist. Standing between the two eras, the Victorian and the Modern, Shaw was able to discern and evaluate various trends of art and literature of the two periods. In fact, he breathed still fresh new life into the thing called art and literature, thereby producing an entirely unique and far more useful and creative view of what was being called the theatre and the art of drama. So, in order to take a judicious and empirical account of his ideas and dramatic art which pursued development and growth, marked by an evolutionary strain, we need to go back to the historical records of the nineteenth and twentieth century British drama. Allardyce Nicoll in his celebrated book *British Drama* traces that the theatre was already deteriorating before the Victorian era. He acknowledges this decline of British drama in his historical survey remarking that "after the time of Sheridan and Goldsmith the Drama rapidly decayed."[1]

Whatever may have been the reasons for the decay, the art and institution of nineteenth century drama was fortunate enough to get the valuable and influential patronage of Queen Victoria and her Court Circle. It was this lucky influence that the general social life of the time started becoming more sober and respectable, in special regard to the Queen's royal and dynamic patronage and concern which paved way for prominent actors to bring their companies to Windsor. Among several genres, melodrama and farces were being performed at the crucial time of the theatrical decline before the Victorian era in the nineteenth century.

It is remarkable, however, that the general tendency of serious drama in the eighteenth century has mostly been classical. Poetic drama could be recognized in the scanty works of Romantics like Shelley, Wordsworth, Keats, Bryon, Robert Southey, leading to Browning and Tennyson of the Victorian period as well. They all had had a good attempt in devoting themselves to "the stage—the desire to invest the drama with poetic fire and thus to revive the glories of the Shakespearean period."[2] But yet at the same time, we are compelled to admit that not one of them had the quality necessary for bringing this laudable ambition to fulfillment. Their failure is thus evident and it was because of their lack of foresight which reminds us of the fact that every true art associated with life is on the path of evolution, which expands and grows. Thus, any attempt to violate the natural process of evolution is bound to end in failure.

Of course, none short of an artist other than one with Shakespeare's superb dramatic skill and an unerring deep understanding and imaginative insight into human nature could delight us with, "All the world's a stage, and all the men and women merely players."[3] Such effective portrayal, needless to say, is found to emanate from "the energy", "the theatrical sense and the air of excitement"[4] that are pivotal to any effective piece of drama of any literary period. In it therefore, comes the germ of truly evolutionary dramatic stance. We hence note that, human life and its institutions are subject to change, progress and evolution and therefore have to undergo the necessary ups and downs on the forward journey. The British playgoers having enough of higher tragic and comic strain perhaps needed a break and a relaxed dramatic environment. The melodramas, farces and extravaganzas which succeeded the romantic poetic-plays became the need of the hour.

The desire to accommodate new themes and fresh plots according to changing tastes led the nineteenth century dramatists to take inspiration from popular contemporary fictions, in terms of adapting the stories and the plots to their melodramatic requirements. The chief sources here, being the works of great and famous novelists like Sir Walter Scott and Charles Dickens. It is noteworthy that it became the same cornerstone of fiction and the novels which indirectly aided Shaw and gave his drama a new way. Shaw from the beginning carried the art of drama to revolutionary trend, bringing it to the maturity that later attained the Himalayan heights.

Nevertheless, as time passed, the taste and aptitude of the playgoers mellowed. Action and thrill related to day-to-day life and incidents drawn from it, such as crime, war, and rebellion, began to be demanded as acceptable themes. The introduction of domestic melodrama associated with the "epoch making Theatre Act of 1843"[5] brought something radically new; the entire realm of domestic melodrama came closer to 'realism', which showed the hard realities of life, and its various seen and unseen problems. Realism, indeed, was a step towards the upcoming art of drama of 1890 till 1920.

The dramatists started showing the signs of a new revival. In 1865 Tom Robertson's *Society* received warm reception followed by *Ours* (1866), *Cast* (1867), *Play* (1868), *Home* (1869), *School* (1869), and *War* (1971), each of which produced altogether a new kind of domestic drama, which was labeled by some commentators as "tea cup and saucer theatre."[6] In fact, it was observed that Robertson's immediate aim behind this new art was to urge the public to bring three fire side concerns, live plots and characters. Sir Arthur Pinnero (1877) made himself distinguished through excellent construction as well as improving earlier efforts at the development of realistic dialogues, preserving "the flavour of actual conversation and gave that conversation an atmosphere of theatrical excitement."[7] As a master of his craft and one of the most significant figures in the dramatic revival which came in the start of twentieth century, Arthur Pinnero, though sometimes suffering from sentimentalism and conventional treatment of characters, remains a pioneer in building the edifice of twentieth century realistic theatre, prophesying the arrival of the Play of Ideas. This prophecy of Sir Pinnero could not be further expanded until the arrival of George Bernard Shaw himself in the late nineteenth century, who under the tremendous influence of the great Norwegian thinker-playwright, Henrik Ibsen, enriched the legacy of the Play of Ideas and took it to new horizons through the versatility of his genius and art. A creative artist and playwright of superb power and originality, coupled with unerring observation and analysis, Shaw directed his artistic and creative efforts towards diagnosing contemporary social evils, as well as giving solutions to them. We may attempt to classify Shaw's dramatic works into three phases. The first being that of social criticism, the middle phase consisting of historical plays, philosophical plays, and post-war plays (increasing his depth of vision), leading to the last group of plays where most among them were designed to indicate the coming times carried with good tidings which extended until the middle of twentieth century.

According to Nicoll, however, it is rather very difficult to define the twentieth century modern British Stage, the context of which is a "motley array of complex and confusing trends."[8] Here, the dominant tendency inside the native theatre was commercialization rather than the production of creative art. One of the great dramatic achievements and tendencies of this period is the definite establishment of prose realistic drama, mostly emphasizing upon the ideas and realistic observation and analysis of contemporary social and moral customs. These realistic prose plays had their own areas to deal with like Problem Plays, the source of which is the native tradition set by Pinnero and Jones based upon the increasing and revolutionary dramatic concept and theory of Ibsen and his successors. The second trend was that of pursuing a more imaginative and poetic objective, and lastly were those who stuck their dramatic theory and practice on comedy. Nevertheless, the problem plays continued to dominate the scene. Here the first and foremost to mention is Bernard Shaw, who with his creative and innovative realistic Problem Plays opened up entirely new avenues for the development of the dramatic art. Quite in line with Shaw, though lesser in art and finish, we cannot but mention the important name of John Galsworthy, who continued in the footsteps of Pinnero and Jones, seeking "theatrical effect from social situation rather than from character."[9] Conclusively, following the same tremendously renewed view of serious and realistic handling of themes, Shaw stands as a "colossus poised to dominate the entire theatre world from the last years of the 19th century on to 1940 and even beyond."[10] No doubt, his dauntless rock-like conviction standing the test of storming opposition always remained behind his criticism and attack of the established and prevailing traditional institutions. It is indeed not simply pricking the bubbles of fanciful and vain glorious practiced norms. Here in this context, as has been pointed out earlier, that Shaw as a dramatist in form and theme, looks so very close to Henrik Ibsen, who in his own time raised the art of drama to a remarkable far reaching and global level; the Theatre of Ideas. In fact, Ibsen pioneered and set a new trend in drama of contemporary social, political and moral life. It was really as if, the history of drama began a new, heralding a remarkable fusion of theme and form. It is likely that Shaw, while starting his Problem Plays did think of Ibsen's success as a dramatist, and being charmed, is reported to have given his fullest agreement. He followed Ibsen's technique and found it pretty useful to employ into his own framework or what came to be known to the theatre world as Problem Plays. Yet the similarities between the two playwrights in respect of management of stage with contemporary setting, admitting discussion, debate and action are obvious. No doubt the *Sunday Sun* called Shaw "The London Ibsen."[11]

Shaw points out, in his preface to *Widower's Houses*, that many of the drama critics have often treated him as a second-hand Ibsen. Shaw in his dramatic criticism, *The Quintessence of Ibsenism*, a controversial essay, has unequivocally confessed that he owes many of his themes and preoccupations and much of his dramatic craft to his Norwegian mentor, Ibsen. Shaw definitely had "an instinctive insight into Ibsen's work"[12] and found Ibsen's ideas very close to his own. His perception of work critically draws a convergence revealing numerous similarities between the revolutionary Ibsen and Shaw himself. However, the interpreters and the critics objected to *The Quintessence of Ibsenism*, condemning the work to be a "brilliantly misconceived piece of criticism which, while helping to gain acceptance for Ibsen on the British stage, butchered him to make a Fabian holiday."[13] Shaw erased their dismay by acknowledging that his primary concern in the book was with Ibsen as a teacher than with Ibsen a poet-dramatist. It is evident that Shaw refused to claim the book as a piece of literary criticism, rather he portrayed it as an account of Ibsen's philosophy of which Ibsen was an exponent. The only purpose in the book was to distill the quintessence of Ibsen's message to Shaw's own age. Shaw strongly believed that Ibsen was a realist whose sole concern was to unveil the gruesome, soaring realities of real life by stripping them of fictitious masks of stringent ideals. According to Shaw, "This was the Ibsen impulse, to get away from idolatry and to get the truth regardless of shattered ideals."[14] Ibsen revolutionized the stage by upsetting the moral values of life by his demanding questions, eventually replacing them by another, rather "opposite set of values."[15]

Shaw owes to Ibsen, to a considerable extent, for giving his plays an indeterminate ending and concluding with discussion rather than action and clear unraveling of a dramatic situation which was undoubtedly the popular form of dramatic presentation in the Victorian England. Their sole objective was to make the challenging ideas more widely available to people in general. Such revolutionary notions came as a shock to the critics who refused to come out of their old, narrow and confined shell of outworn yardstick to evaluate genuine pieces of art and theatre. Therefore, the critics ended up refusing to call their drama as drama. But to remember, a great artist is obliged to pursue an evolutionary trend in his art with some certain and definite higher goals that could be effective and problem solving. The art and artifice are just tools, instrument towards evaluating, diagnosing and setting the various issues of man and society, so that such tools and instruments eventually become one with the message. In fact, the rejection of the stereotype dramatization of obsolete ideas pregnant with hypocritical goodness of society was beyond the general and narrow understanding of most of the contemporary critics and interpreters. However, Eric Bentley, one of the most eminent and comprehensive of Shaw's critics, asserts:

> Shaw was challenging the basic conventions of character on the Victorian Stage. And anyone who challenges the current convention of the stage is asking for different methods from his actors. If he practices what he preaches,

> his work must in the very nature of things—habit being, what it is—be declared 'not drama.' It was this deviation from the conventions that linked Shaw's causes with Ibsen's.[16]

The link between Ibsen and Shaw lies in the fact that they were both criticizing the society and its norms. Shaw regarded Ibsen as essentially a social critic as is evident from his following observation:

> The happiest and truest epithet that has yet been applied to Ibsen drama in this country came from Mr. Clement Scott when he said that Ibsen was Suburban... Suburbanity at present means modern civilization.... And this suburban life, except in so far as it is totally vegetable and undramatic, is the life depicted by Ibsen.[17]

It is quite well known that Ibsen's *Doll's House* offended the so-called sophisticated English audiences. They were shocked to see Nora's act of deserting her domestic obligations. Practically, breaking the bonds of convention in a self-created society was not accepted at all. They could not bear to see the blasphemy, Ibsen was teaching their women, hence patriarchal society revolted against the play in the theatres. Ibsen replied this uproar through his next play *The Ghost*. Here an unhappy married woman is tied to her unfaithful husband and his gloomy household and syphilis affected son with disastrous consequences. Ibsen chooses a priest to speak on behalf of the rigid society. Mrs. Alving is constantly reminded by the priest of her monogamous obligations to her husband, sending her back to him. The motive behind this play was to bring out the gruesome consequences that the rigid and dogmatic social-moral norms often lead to. Many of Ibsen's and Shaw's households project the tragic state of affairs generated by the friction between an older order and a newer spirit. Something of the similar story lives behind Shaw's Mrs. Dudgeon in his famous play *The Devil's Disciple*. Mrs. Dudgeon accuses the minister of the gospel for having destroyed her life by binding her into the bond of matrimony with the man she did not love. Accusing Eli Hawkins and Anderson, the two religious masters, she complains that, "He warned me and strengthened me against my heart, and made me marry a Godfearing man—as he thought. What else but that disciple has made me the woman I am?"[18] We know much of her person already as in the very beginning of the play. Shaw describes her face as, "even at its best, is grimly trenched by the channels into which the barren forms and observances of the dead Puritanism can pen a bitter temper and a fierce pride."[19] The rigid Puritanism and its outcomes have gradually made her son Dick, an apparent devil's disciple.

Ibsen and Shaw were both sailing in the troubled waters. Shaw realized the need to write the following lines, where he made some crucial consequential remarks referring to Ghost, also highlighting Ibsen's universal appeal:

> Mrs. Alving is nobody in particular; she is a typical figure of the experienced intelligent woman who in passing from first to the last quarter of the hour of history called the nineteenth century, has discovered how appallingly opportunities were wasted, morals perverted and instincts corrupted, not only sometimes, not only by the vices she was taught to abhor in her youth, but by the virtues it was her pride and uprightness to maintain.[20]

Whatsoever is said by Shaw is undeniable and difficult to sweep under the carpet. These hollow values have been deeply penetrated in mind as well as souls of people. Therefore, we can now rightly believe that Ibsen truly "depicted the life of his time and made use of the ideas of his time."[21] Shaw again has a word of praise for Henrik Ibsen. He rightly acknowledges:

> He (Ibsen) is master of the situation, this man of genius;... when any person objects to an Ibsen play because it does not hold mirror up to his own mind, I can only remind him that a horse might make exactly the same objection.[22]

Shaw uses his dramatic art in order to modify old ideas and to solve the existing contemporary problems by staging the slice of life with his wide range of living dramatic personae in his brilliant series of drama. His proper understanding of Ibsen helps to collate the two ideologies and presentations. After having felt and recognized, that evil is rampant, Shaw began to demolish the convention and outmoded followed paths. Shaw commences his dramatic journey with the determination to deal with the real problems of life and society. For this reason he makes a sharp distinction between realism and idealism, focusing the clash between the two, with realism taking an upper hand over idealism, sentimentalism, romanticism, and capitalism. Shaw's satire was sharp enough to penetrate into every aspect of life and institutions, critically and logically diagnosing the maladies but also with solutions. Shaw's first play, *Widower's Houses*, attacks the notion of personal righteousness and idealism. Shaw's campaign against idealism, his social realism and truth are again like Ibsen's. *The Enemy of the People* reflexes Ibsen's demonstration of the fact that, there are no absolute truths for "...truth is in...constant flux."[23] And of course this truth, Shaw finds and presents very effectively. Like Nietzsche, he seeks to investigate "those judgments of values, Good and Evil, to discover what intrinsic value they possess in themselves."[24] The truth is connected to conduct which must rightly justify itself by its effect upon life, and not by simply adhering to any dogmatic rule, because life is in "constant flux." Shaw's aim, then, "is not necessarily to overturn existing institutions and traditions, but to get men to think for themselves—or at least to secure freedom to think and speak for those who want to...."[25]

Shaw with his own experiences interprets life accordingly. He mainly deals with the hidden realities because the visualized actions of people are nothing but half truth. He speculates not only the literary pieces for this purpose but the actual movements of living people. As Shaw was a realist and a naturalist, he interacted with the problems and issues of contemporary society in the same light. He could not join hands with the idealist, the sect he was unable to tolerate. He also draws a sharp distinction between an idealist and a realist. In his *Quintessence of Ibsenism*, he recognizes the meanings of the two words idealist and realist. A person, who conceals facts just to make them look pleasant, is an idealist, and a realist is the man who toils to perceive future possibilities. H.C. Duffin explains in detail the aforementioned meanings of the two words. His research reveals:

> An idealist is one who, having obtained from—literature, the pulpit, home-teaching, or his own imagination—a false

> notion of how things ought to be, painfully that they are not, supposes that this is due to some sinful-shortcoming on the part of himself and the other people concerned in the situation and endeavors to force his nature and theirs and the situation itself to fit the "ideal" as he has conceived it, the realist looks straight at facts, and believes that it is only by building upon facts as they are that "future possibilities" can be realized.[26]

But Shaw does not discredit the laws and principles completely. He only tries to insist that every issue must be judged on its very own merits instead of some presupposed and preconceived principles of right and wrong. Idealism along with sentimentalism and other notions only hold life and actions within the boundaries of confinement that stops growth and evolution. According to Allardyce Nicoll:

> In his plays, Shaw was constantly making fun or was more seriously attacking Sentimentalism attitudes; but the sentimentalism he disliked was what might be called the unconscious or stereotyped Sentimental attitude which so frequently intruded and still intrudes into realistic plays.[27]

Shaw has no patience with sentimentalism and hollow sentimentalism because firstly, mere sentiment is superficial and blind to reality and realism and therefore, is incapable of comprehending situations of life or problems and issues associated with it. Sentimentalism is the result of superstitious beliefs which always tries to escape from the realistic appraisal of things. Since Shaw is a realist, he feels pressed not only to investigate and diagnose issues and challenges of man and social institutions, but also is anxious to find solutions to them. He has got to be very hard on sentimentalism and therefore adopts what is true and real. His art and technique, therefore, serve him like the surgeon's knife, which though apparently sharp and merciless, means to cut and cure the patient of the diseases. Shaw tried to cure people of the disease of mind and thought by making them aware of sentimentalism, romanticism, idealism, and sensuousness as major hurdles in growth and advancement. Shaw's themes are not purely realistic, they not only deal with social realities, but they are often concerned with the very rudiments of human nature. We can include a number of plays like *Major Barbara*, *Candida*, *The Devil's Disciple*, *How He Lied to Her Husband*, *Mrs. Warren's Profession*, *Arms and the Man* and the list continues. All these involve a tussle between the so-called moralistic values and realistic approaches. The realistic approach towards capitalism and socialism reveals the truths and realities as well as condemns romanticism to the very core. *Arms and the Man*, shatters Raina's false sense of a romantic hero worship in her fiancé, Sergius Saranoff. On practical terms, she accepts her "Chocolate Cream Soldier", Bluntschilli for matrimonial tie. The anti-climax in the play clears an important point that laws are to be kept when proved useful, and, broken when violated. This is best exemplified when Louka, the maid servant tears the hypocritical morals of her master, Sergius. It is the conduct that has to justify itself upon life, rather than confinement to any rigid rules. Shaw denies the notion that supreme goodness is supreme martyrdom. It means that man is great not by his nature alone but by his governance of thought and action. Shaw in the preface to *Major Barbara* upholds the notion that, "It is quite useless to declare that all men are born free if you deny that they are born good."[28]

Humans are fortunately blessed with conscience as well as liberty. Liberty which is the highest achievement of man can only be attained at the cost of responsibility. This responsibility falls upon every man and woman heading towards betterment of not an individual alone but for humanity at large. Here we are reminded of Ibsen's quotation which calls for the unification of humanity, "We are the members of one another and though the strongest man is he who stands alone, the man who is standing alone for his own sake solely is literally an idiot."[29] A parallel understanding is sought in Shaw's preface to *Major Barbara*, where he believes that every man and woman has to be a part of this diverse world. Shaw says that, "He must either share the world's guilt or go to another planet. He must save the world's honor if he is to save his own."[30]

The ability to face the truth of life is a secret of the art of living because "the lot of the man who sees life truly and thinks about it romantically is Despair."[31] For the reconstruction of the world, there is an urgent need to first shed off the preconceived ideas, high sounding but hollow morals of man and society because "Nature will not dance to his moralist-made tunes."[32] Shaw does not set the first example of being a revolutionary artist. Many men of letters before Shaw have shocked the public with their revolutionary and daring views. Shaw definitely agrees to these prints on the sand of time. He himself reports:

> Swift, accepting our system of morals and religion, delivered the inevitable verdict of that system on us through the mouth of the king of Brobdingnag, and described Man as the Yahoo, shocking his superior the horse by his every action. Strindberg, the only genuinely Shakespearian modern dramatist, shews that the female Yahoo, measured by romantic standards, is viler than her male dupe and slave. I respect these resolute tragi-comedians: they are logical and faithful: they force you to face the fact that you must either accept their conclusions as valid (in which case it is cowardly to continue living) or admit that their way of judging conduct is absurd.[33]

A very fine example can be traced from Shaw's play *How He Lied to Her Husband* where the young Henry, the romantic dreamer miserably awakes, "But oh! the misgiving at the first stir of consciousness! the stab of reality! The prison walls of the bedroom! the bitter, bitter disappointment of waking! And this time! Oh, this time I thought I was awake."[34] Arora, a middle-aged married woman and Henry's beloved calmly explains to him, "It's very nice of you to live with me in a dream...but I cant help my husband having disagreeable realities, can I?"[35] It is alright for people to dream, as long as eyes are closed, as for the laws of nature are quite obedient to their own. Shaw's *Man and Superman* echoes in the hell seen through Don Juan:

> The earth is a nursery in which men and women play at being heroes and heroines, saints and sinners; but they are dragged down from their fool's paradise by their bodies: hunger and cold and thirst, age and decay and disease, death above all, make them slaves of reality.[36]

In order to save oneself, an individual strives to overcome the bitter reality of "hunger and cold and thirst, age and decay and disease,"[37] but definitely faces death, the inevitable. Unless his aim is to save the world, he cannot save himself even with the help of the powers of capitalism and plutocracy. Shaw remains very satiric to these two. According to Shaw, most of the recurring maladies in the West have been because of capitalism and plutocracy which are responsible for producing poverty. He campaigns that every man is to be given enough so as to live upon, if we dare to campaign against poverty. Shaw consciously calls himself a socialist. Harry Trench, the sentimental idealist, in *Widower's Houses* very bitterly realizes that people around him become the victim of the octopus of capitalism. Though sympathetic to the causes of the under-privileged, he is disgusted to learn about his finance Blanche, whose refinement and culture is derived from the dire poverty and tireless oppression. Dr. Trench here has been portrayed as every man who discovers that capitalism has permeated to the very bottom of society; nobody is free from its polluting perversions. Shaw, thus, shatters the false pride and dignity as maintained by the people. This shallowness of affected victims, both by idealism and capitalism, are seriously depicted in *Mrs. Warren's Profession*. Shaw approaches the problem of prostitution from the socialist and feminist point of view. It makes the case elegant and practical that selling one's body in capitalist society is a better deal for women than working in factories. Mrs. Warren gives detailed explanation without apologies to her daughter, Vivie, whose college education was financed from her mother's profit. Shaw intends to demonstrate the under payment and ill-treatment of women, leaving no other options but only to generate prostitution. Shaw tells us in his preface that, "prostitution is caused, not by female depravity and male licentiousness, undervaluing and overworking women so shamefully that the poorest of them are forced to resort to prostitution to keep body and soul together."[38] Shaw denies in his comment in 1905 about *Mrs. Warren's Profession* that his business was to impart moral lessons. He wrote, "my business is to interpret life by taking events occurring at haphazard in experiences and sorting them out so as to, show their real significance and interrelation."[39]

Capitalism generated plutocracy on one hand and poverty on the other. It is by solving the problems of poverty, the worst and a malignant disease, along with the issues of plutocracy a ray of hope can be visible. Capitalism and plutocracy are the two extreme stumbling blocks in the progress of any nation. Shaw here suggests some proper measures after having diagnosed the root cause of maximum maladies. "The first duty of every citizen is to insist on having money on reasonable terms" and further he adds, "and this demand is not complied with by giving four men three shillings each for ten or twelve hours' drudgery and one man a thousand pounds for nothing."[40] Unless every man is given enough to live upon, the possibility to fight against the "malignant disease of poverty"[41] is definitely beyond our reach. The importance lies in ensuring that the money is earned. So where does Andrew Undershaft in *Major Barbara* go wrong? His article of faith recognized, "Money the first need and in poverty the vilest sin of man and society."[42] Shaw reveals to the readers in his preface to *Major Barbara* that he was not the first dramatist or a man of letters to realize the importance of money. Samuel Butler in the later half of the nineteenth century had recognized the importance and necessity of morality of religion and of money. But it is very sad that nobody could realize the important message given by Butler. In a lamenting tone, Shaw writes, "Really, the English do not deserve to have great men. They allowed Butler to die practically unknown."[43] Coming back to the play, Andrew Undershaft's intelligent daughter, Major Barbara's ego is deeply wounded on her knowledge that the source of her Salvation Army's fund was provided by her father's business of manufacturing and supplying arms and explosives for warfare. But it hardly takes her much time to recognize the rampant evils and the universal hypocrisy. She finally returns to colours. Shaw, observing the issues on practical terms, is disgusted with the sources of money earned. In fact, all the money throughout the country comes from rent, interest, profit. Hence, all is linked with crime, prostitution, disease, and others and these are nothing but "the evil fruits of poverty."[44] Hence, every penny is tainted. But it gives "a very severe shock to earnest young souls when some dramatic instance of the taint first makes them conscious of it."[45] Shaw is almost on the verge of losing his temper, and states that, "it is exceedingly difficult to make people realize that an evil is an evil."[46] But Shaw can be seen to be successful in making people realize that an evil is an evil. His popularity and box office prove the same. In his *Preface on Bosses*, Shaw admits:

> The law is equal before all of us, but we are not at all equal before the law. Virtually, there is one law for the rich and another for the poor, one law for the cunning and another for the simple, one law for the forceful and another for the feeble, one law for the ignorant and another for the learned, one law for the brave and another for the timid, and within family limits one law for the parent and no law at all for the child.[47]

Reflecting on the play *The Devil's Disciple*, we find that people can see evils in a person like Dick Dudgeon, who appears to be deviating from the norms of the conventional society. Shaw names his play after Dick, the main character, who has acquired from his community the title 'The Devil's Disciple'. Dick has been brought up in an environment of a dying Puritan religion. "In such homes the young Puritan finds himself starved of religion, which is the most clamorous need of his nature."[48] Dick goes against the selfishness and hatred of his mother and the world around him. "He, thus becomes, like all genuinely religious men, a reprobate and an outcast,"[49] says Shaw. A slight mention of the reprobate's name "jars on the moral sense of the family."[50] But Dick is no ordinary devil, on his encounter with his family members, he starts unmasking the hidden devils in each of the present characters. On behalf of Shaw, Dick unfolds the hypocrisy and immortality they are occupied with. We have biggest laugh for the ironical moves made by the young sentimentally romantic minister's wife, Judith, who moves away from the Devil Disciple's neighbourhood, "holding her skirt instinctively as if to save it from contamination."[51] She is finally caught in the dense truth of life and realism. Judith falls in love with the so-called "the wicked, dissolute, godless,"[52] when he exchanges the hangman's noose with Judith's husband, Anderson, the minister. Critics questioned Dick, the blackguard's reason for saving the life of a minister who was not his friend. They themselves were impatient and provided the answer on their own timid understanding, declaring that he saved the minister's life, "because he is redeemed by love."[53] But to remember that Dick was not a romantic hero, he was a puritan of puritans from within. He was "a man impassioned only for saving grace, and not to be led or turned by wife or mother, Church or State, pride of life or lust of the flesh."[54] Shaw adds that, "he would have done as much for any stranger—that the law of his own nature, and no interest nor lust whatsoever, forbad him to carry out that the hangman's noose should be taken off his neck only to be put on another man's."[55] Don Juan in *Man and Superman* reminds us "Remember: the devil is not so black as he is painted."[56]

There are numerous examples of such incidents in the works of other men of letters as well. John Bunyan summed up his stories with the possibility of entering hell from the gates of heaven and vice versa. William Blake called his angel a devil and the devil an angel, as well as, a redeemer. Nietzsche's writing on such topics offended people. Our dramatist, Bernard Shaw, in spite of the continued controversies, to which he was perhaps habitual, found desperate need to write and stage *The Devil's Disciple*, at the end of the nineteenth century because, "the age was visibly pregnant with it."[57] Shaw also agrees and clarifies that *The Devil's Disciple* has a novelty, "that novelty is not any invention of my own, but simply the novelty of the advanced thought of my day."[58] It was indeed the ultimate necessity to wake up the slumbering lots. Dick Dudgeon readily accepts sacrifice and martyrdom. This confused the critics beyond their wits as they could not understand the way Dick described himself as a staunch follower of the devil, though there are plenty of situations and incidents contradicting this description within the play from the beginning till the very end. One of the critics still described Dick as "A finished scoundrel", to which Shaw promptly replied, "This is worth recording as an example of the extent to which the moral sense remains dormant in people, who are content with the customary formulas for respectable conduct."[59] Here, we can trace the similar situation but in historical context from *Saint Joan*. Ladvenu narrates to Warwick:

> When the fire crept round us, and she (Joan) saw that if I held the cross before her I should be burnt myself, she warned me to get down and save myself. My lord: a girl who could think of another's danger in such a moment was not inspired by the devil...I firmly believe that her Savior appeared to her then in His tenderest glory. She called to Him and died.[60]

Although Saint Joan has been defeated and burned in her life time, the history remains witness to the fact that she has survived as an inspiration for generations to come. Joan's final cry, "how long, O lord how long?" focuses our attention to the perhaps glorious future. Therefore, Ladvenu announces "This is not the end for her, but the beginning."[61]

The motive behind Shaw's plays is to propagate his revolutionary thoughts and ideas, as well as connecting the past, present and future. Therefore, Shaw portrays the realities of life on stage. He suggests that, "life has its realities behind its shows: the theatre has nothing but its shows."[62] What defines an era is the sum of individuals and their attitudes including economic, social, political, religious, literary, intellectual and also critical. Though Shaw sees a "distinction between one epoch and another, there is a continuity in human experience that creates links between different historical periods,"[63] for human nature is always the same everywhere. Bernard Shaw, through his long, fertile and progressive journey, discovers later in his historical plays that, "the great man is a person who incarnates an idea, so his conception of a historical epoch is a period of time that embodies an idea."[64] However, the changes have always been needed for progress and evolution. Historical changes occur, when thought is embodied in men and women of action, like Saint Joan and Julius Caesar. But thought when inactive and detached from the sphere of action remains impotent. Thought, the pre-eminent, is the preparatory condition for any historical change. Thought is but ideas that Shaw is emphasizing. J.L. Wisenthal in *Shaw's Sense of History* discovered that "the term historical means more to Shaw than 'factual.' Shaw regards ideas rather than events as the essence of history, and his dramatic practice reflects this attitude."[65] Shaw himself admits that his historical plays were "easy to write because the facts are a gift: all that has to be done is to supply the ideas, and the people personifying the ideas."[66] We must ponder here for historical truth, similar to any other kind of truth that is not necessarily a matter of fact. It is, in fact, the question of interpretation and which is nothing but imagination.

Shaw, in the year 1894, imparted an important statement in a newspaper interview, regarding his dramatic historiography. His reply is worth the record to the question whether he considered a historical play as a force to be substantially accurate to facts or not:

> Not more so that not any other sort of play. Historical facts are not a bit more sacred than any other class of facts. In making a play out of them you must adapt them to the stage and that alters them at once, more or less. Why you cannot even write a history without adapting the facts to the condition of literary narrative. Which are in some respects much more distorting than the dramatic conditions of representation on the stage. Things do not happen in the form of stories or dramas; and since they must be told in such forms, all reports, even by eyewitnesses, all histories, all stories, all dramatic representations are only attempts to arrange the facts in a thinkable, intelligent, interesting form that is when they are not more or less intentional efforts to hide the truth, as they very often are.[67]

One of the most prominent aspects of Shaw's treatment of historical characters differs from the other by dramatic methods of presentation. It is worthy to note that his revolutionary treatment has not only dealt with the domain of the characters signifying common men and women, but he is observed to make required amendments even in his historical characters. Shaw often makes his dramatic personae much more cautious of their existing epochs, than their historical originals could have been. King Charles is portrayed in a very different light in *King Charles Golden Days*. Shaw's aim here is to set the exact records as a historical dramatist. "He demonstrates the error and misconception of all previous literary treatments of the subject and the play itself is offered as a corrective."[68] On the preface to the play on King Charles, Shaw writes:

> Unfortunately the vulgarity of his reputation as a Solomonic polygamist has not only obscured his political ability, but eclipsed the fact that he was the best of husbands. Catherine of Braganza, his wife, has been made to appear a nobody, and Castlemaine, his concubine, almost a great historical figure. When you have seen my play you will not make that mistake, and may congratulate yourself on assisting at an act of historical justice.[69]

Shaw claims to attempt for historical accuracy in, *Good King Charles's Golden Days*. He demands both the readers and the playgoers to avoid making mistake with historical records, because his *Good King Charles* offers "historical justice" and his *Saint Joan* also aims for historical accuracy. Shaw also had a sharp eye for historical parallels. *Saint Joan* imparts "an element of the history lesson," "and one of the dramatist's pedagogical techniques is to make his characters more cautious of their epoch than their historical originals would have therefore been,"[70] observes J.L. Wisenthal. Shaw, in a letter to Cockrell about *Saint Joan* explained his concept of idea and people carrying the ideas that gain upper hand. He writes:

> I am not inordinately proud of it. You see, it was very easy to write: the materials were there, and even the historical manufacture had been worked over by so many hands that I am only the author in the sense that Michael Angelo was the architect of St. Peter's. Ruskin and Morris and all the painters were on the job before me: I have had only to pull it together and fit it in.[71]

Shaw's inclination towards historical subjects has deep roots in his high appreciation of medieval art and pre-Raphaelite brotherhood as well as the entire civilization that produced it, which is very much like William Morris's and Ruskin's. He argued that "the superiority of Middle Ages is owing to the medieval world's superiority as a society". The deterioration of "religious art" through sixteenth and nineteenth century was only due to the "eclipse of religion by science and commerce" than the wit of the "artistic faculty."[72] Shaw recollects, "In autumn of 1894 I spent a few weeks in Florence, where I occupied myself with the religious art of the Middle Ages and its destruction by the Renascence."[73] On his home coming, he felt the time was absolute for a pre-Raphaelite drama and hence, we find the birth of his fifth play *Candida*. Here, Morrel, a Christian Society clergyman is held against the Capitalist Bergess. The action, debate and the conflict culminates in the poet's, Marchbank, running away from the domestic contentment to seek refuge into the nights in search of higher destiny. Shaw thereby, exerts his primacy of religious impulse. *Candida* is again a blend of many flavours, reflecting upon Shaw's admiration for medieval era.

Shaw holds similar views as those of the historian, Thomas Carlyle's, where both firmly hold on to the superiority of the Middle Ages, revealing the inadequacy of the present time. Shaw has shown a clear distinction between the feudal aristocracy in the Middle Ages and the plutocracy of the present time. It is observed that Shaw, like Carlyle, Ruskin and Morris is positive towards the medieval age, particularly as an alternative to the debased present. Shaw argues that:

> All that about Dark Ages and the barbarous Middle Ages is a modern hallucination, partly pious, partly commercial. There never were any Dark ages, except in the imagination of the Blind Ages. Look at the cathedrals and their houses; and terminus at Euston and the Gambetta monument.[74]

Shaw has taken care to reflect this attitude through his works. We find him very generously telling Sydney Cockerell that Ruskin and Morris, including all the painters were on the job before him regarding the historical background of his plays. His *Saint Joan* is reflective of the tussle between his own protestant background and the Victorian England. In the play, the attention is on Protestantism, "that great self-assertion of the growing spirit of man," as contrary to the renaissance, "the vulgar exploitation in the artistic professions."[75] For Shaw the nineteenth century is quite distant from the parliamentary democracy, it is an age of capitalism, which is nothing but "the robber's road to ruin," as also viewed by Ruskin, Morris and Dickens. It is the outcome of Shaw's peregrination that he saw things differently from the generally accepted views. He calls the nineteenth century, the wickedest of all the centuries, worst of times and a real dark age. Shaw said, "The nineteenth century, which believed itself to be the climax of civilization, of Liberty, Equality, and Fraternity, was convicted by Karl Marx of being the worst and wickedest on record; and the twentieth, not yet half through, has been ravaged by two so-called world wars culminating in the atrocity of the atomic bomb."[76] A study of *Saint Joan* reveals Shaw's disgust with the First World War, which brought the greatest transformation and disillusioning experience in Shaw's own life. The need for a clear solution in the misty environment was delivered through the sublimity of *Saint Joan*.

Shaw's revolutionary thoughts were built upon a keen observation of things around, coupled with an inner creative urge and longing "to grasp this sorry Scheme of Things entire."[77] It is like a hurricane or the raging storm that Shaw, like P.B. Shelley, would like to bring about. His radical transformation will do away with all the rotten, sick and corroding chain of pride and prejudice that hold up the face of reality. Secondly, he would like to offer reordering and reorganization of the existing social, political, economic orders, with assurance of leaving behind no human institution untouched. It was indeed an unprecedented and an extremely arduous project for the dramatist to undertake, based upon his tremendous creative powers. For this he had to begin a satirist, a destroyer working on contemporary scene, invariably, maintaining the spontaneous sense of unity and coherence in respect of dramatic revolution in the realm of art and ideas. Shaw admits that, "the artist-philosophers are the only sort of artists I take quite seriously, will be no news to you."[78] Like Shelley's 'West Wind' Shaw is a "destroyer" only to be a "preserver." His satires with all his wit and humor, art and artistry lead to some benevolent social order. His later plays from *Man and Superman*, *Back to Methuselah*, *Saint Joan*, and to *Apple Cart*, are evident of this coherence. He is no doubt one of the few writers who had the courage to think of tomorrow and to mend and prepare the world to meet the challenges of the future without the least indulgence in what is called living in the fool's paradise. It is Shaw's realistic approach and sheer dedication to his mission, as is with every great writer that he does not mean to impose things. His works rather render effective appeal to the readers, offering natural spirit of choice and judgment. Addressing Mr. Arthur Bingham Walkley in *Epistle Dedicatory* in his masterly achievement, *Man and Superman*, he in fact, conveys his message to the entire reading world saying that, "Its profits, like its labor, belong to me: its morals, its manners, its philosophy, its influence on the young, are for you to justify."[79]

Darwin's theory of natural selection which according to Shaw "might have had as a sub-title 'The revelation of a method' by which all the appearances of intelligent design in the universe may have been produced by pure accidents,"[80] seems to contradict rather than offer a clue to Shaw's Life Force. This Life Force takes the universe as a result not of chance or accident, but rather as a purposeful design behind it, which gets its full focus in correlating to the spiritual and divine base of creation. It also hands over the brilliant, spiritual legacy of the 'Divine Trust' to the future generation. Tanner, who comes very close to Shaw's philosophy of life, in *Man and Superman* Act-1 undertakes Shaw's sportsmanship declaring to Ann, that "I shatter creeds and demolish idols,"[81] "the creeds and the idols," so mentioned here is symbolic of old lifeless and dead institutions. He explains to her that his action is for a purpose and for the sake of evolution. He also makes a sharp distinction between construction and destruction. "Construction cumbers the ground with institutions made by busybodies. Destruction clears it and gives us breathing space and liberty,"[82] only for a purpose and for the sake of evolution. We find Alfred Tennyson also echoing the same views in his *Morte D'Arthur*:

> Old order changeth yielding place to new,
> God fulfills himself in many ways,
> Lest one good custom should corrupt the world.[83]

Tennyson seems to reflect some divine scheme behind birth and evolution, which is destined to be the law of nature in the form of blessing for man and society. Shaw's concept of evolution, professing the arrival of Superman, can be said to belong to Tennyson's similar perception. But with the exception that Shaw goes ahead of him in putting the process to culminate in the Superman, who is to be the result of the evolution of man, "The great central purpose of breeding the race: ay, breeding it to heights now deemed superhuman."[84] With Shaw, it is always the higher purpose, aspiring for the attainment of richer future for the humanity at large. It is this elevated goal that determines, enriches, and makes it poised for fresh life. It is through Don Juan in the hell scene that Shaw gives his judgment on the higher purpose, evolution and fulfillment of life, "Were I not possessed with the purpose beyond my own I had better be a ploughman than a philosopher; for the ploughman lives as long as a philosopher.... This is because a philosopher is in the grip of Life Force. This Life Force says to him…must thou strive to do for me until thou diest, when I will make another brain and another philosopher to carry on the work."[85] In *Back to Methuselah*, Franklyn warns, that "The force behind evolution, call it what you like, is determined to solve the problem of civilization; and if it cannot do it through us, it will produce more capable agents. You and I are not God's last word: God can still create. If you cannot do His work He will produce some being who can."[86] It is the idea behind the creation of human species that Shaw is hinting at, where men and women are the agents for taking the civilization towards progress of thought and ideas. Shavian drama is thus seen to thrive and sustain on this remarkable evolutionary trend for the invariably brilliant theme and mission, termed the attainment of the Superman by its author.

Though it is hard to discern and distinguish Shaw's dramatic flow and stream it into various chronological periods and try to confine and captivate them into clear-cut periods, at best a thematic classification is possible. Having attained fuller maturity and development in dramatic art, Shaw made many important shifts and alterations, all desired and needed towards a purposeful design and aspiring to evolve into a wider range of dramatic achievements, Shaw's development of dramatic art underwent "change of theme from the particular to the general, from the contemporary scene to the future, and of attitude from satiric and destructive to the philosophic and constructive, from the materialist to the mythic."[87]

Armed with the tremendous, innovative, and creative potentials, Shavian drama is inclusive of its art and forceful ideas developed and flowed in spontaneous and evolutionary stream, remaining graceful and matchless perhaps for centuries to come. Thus, what looks significant in this context is that art and ideas, in order to serve, survive and flourish, must associate it with the changing realities and challenges of real life situations which demand a thorough evolutionary base and concept. Evolutionary concept needs to be flowing, dynamic, organized and planned as against Erasmus Darwin's attempt to trace the pretext of "chance" and "accidents" behind it. The fact is that Shaw's dramatic art built up on his unique techniques of paradoxes, wit and humor, baffling repartees, all converging on his rarest gift of debates and discussions are echoed through his memorable and engaging forewords. His art would not be effective enough without his extraordinary evolutionary concept of what art should do and how it should co-ordinate with the changing context of life, its stresses and storms, crying for an answer and a solution.

Notes

1. Allardyce Nicoll. *British Drama*. New Delhi: Doaba House, 2005. p. 200.
2. *Ibid.*, pp. 219-20.
3. William Shakespeare. *As You Like It*. ed. Vinita Chandra. Delhi: Worldview, 2000. p. 57.
4. Allardyce Nicoll. *British Drama*. New Delhi: Doaba House, 2005. p. 220.
5. *Ibid.*, p. 226.
6. *Ibid.*, p. 231.
7. *Ibid.*, p. 236.
8. *Ibid.*, p. 247.
9. *Ibid.*, pp. 254-55.
10. *Ibid.*, p. 280.
11. Shaw. *Preface of Bernard Shaw*. London: Hamilton, 1965. p. 704.
12. Shaw. "Introduction." *Major Critical Essays*. England, Middlesex: Penguin, 1986. p. 11.
13. *Ibid.*
14. *Ibid.*

15. Rahmat Jahan. *The Ibsen-Shaw Kinship*. Calcutta: Writers Workshop, 2002. p. 24.
16. Eric Bentley. *Bernard Shaw*. London, 1950. p. 166.
17. Shaw. *The Quintessence of Ibsenism*. Boston: Benjamin R. Tucker. 1891. p. 124.
18. Shaw. "The Devil's Disciple." ed. Dan H.L. *The Bodely Head Bernard Shaw Collected Plays with their Prefaces*. Vol. 2. London: Max Reinhardt, 1980. p. 62.
19. *Ibid.*, p. 53.
20. H.L. Mencken. "The Introduction." *Plays of Ibsen*. New York: Modern Library, 1950. p. xiii.
21. *Ibid.*
22. Shaw. *Major Critical Essays*. England, Middlesex: Penguin, 1986. p. 257.
23. Rolf Fjelde. "Ibsen's Conception of Truth." *Ibsen: A Collection of Critical Essays*. Englewood Cliffs, N.J.: Prentice-Hall, 1965. p. 19.
24. H.C. Duffin. *Quintessence of Bernard Shaw*. Delhi: Doaba House, 1959. p. 2.
25. *Ibid.*
26. *Ibid.*, p. 7.
27. Allardyce Nicoll. *British Drama*. New Delhi: Doaba House, 2005. p. 288.
28. Shaw. "Preface." *Major Barbara*. ed. Dan H.L. *The Bodely Head Bernard Shaw Collected Plays with their Prefaces*. Vol. 3. London: Max Reinhardt, 1971. p. 48.
29. Shaw. *Major Critical Essays*. England, Middlesex: Penguin, 1986. p. 125.
30. Shaw. "Major Barbara". ed. Dan H.L. *The Bodely Head Bernard Shaw Collected Plays with their Prefaces*. Vol. 3. London: Max Reinhardt, 1971. p. 36.
31. Shaw. "Preface." *The Devil's Disciple*. ed. Dan H.L. *The Bodely Head Bernard Shaw Collected Plays with their Prefaces*. Vol. 2. London: Max Reinhardt, 1980. p. 37.
32. *Ibid.*
33. *Ibid.*, p. 38.
34. Shaw. "How He Lied to Her Husband." ed. Dan H.L. *The Bodely Head Bernard Shaw Collected Plays with their Prefaces*. Vol. 2. London: Max Reinhardt, 1980. p. 1040.
35. *Ibid.*, p. 1034.

36. Shaw. "Man and Superman." ed. Dan H.L. *The Bodely Head Bernard Shaw Collected Plays with their Prefaces*. Vol. 2. London: Max Reinhardt, 1980. p. 650.
37. *Ibid.*
38. Shaw. "Mrs. Warren's Profession." ed. Dan H.L. *The Bodely Head Bernard Shaw Collected Plays with their Prefaces*. Vol. 1. London: Max Reinhardt, 1971. p. 219.
39. *Ibid.*, p. 362.
40. Shaw. "Preface." *Major Barbara*. ed. Dan H.L. *The Bodely Head Bernard Shaw Collected Plays with their Prefaces*. Vol. 3. London: Max Reinhardt, 1971. p. 31.
41. *Ibid.*
42. *Ibid.*, p. 32.
43. *Ibid.*
44. *Ibid.*, p. 35.
45. *Ibid.*
46. *Ibid.*, p. 23.
47. Shaw. "Preface." Millionairess. ed. Dan H.L. *The Bodely Head Bernard Shaw Collected Plays with their Prefaces*. Vol. 6. London: Max Reinhardt, 1973. p. 846.
48. Shaw. "Preface." *The Devil's Disciple*. ed. Dan H.L. *The Bodely Head Bernard Shaw Collected Plays with their Prefaces*. Vol. 2. London: Max Reinhardt, 1980. p. 33.
49. *Ibid.*
50. *Ibid.*, p. 69.
51. *Ibid.*, p. 71.
52. *Ibid.*, p. 59.
53. *Ibid.*, p. 34.
54. *Ibid.*, p. 35.
55. *Ibid.*
56. Shaw. "Man and Superman." ed. Dan H.L. *The Bodely Head Bernard Shaw Collected Plays with their Prefaces*. Vol. 2. London: Max Reinhardt, 1980. p. 643.
57. Shaw. "Preface." *The Devil's Disciple*. ed. Dan H.L. *The Bodely Head Bernard Shaw Collected Plays with their Prefaces*. Vol. 2. London: Max Reinhardt, 1980. p. 34.
58. *Ibid.*, p. 32.
59. *Ibid.*, pp. 36-37.

60. Shaw. "Saint Joan." ed. Dan H.L. *The Bodely Head Bernard Shaw Collected Plays with their Prefaces*. Vol. 6. London: Max Reinhardt, 1973. p. 189.
61. *Ibid.*
62. Shaw. "Preface." *The Devil's Disciple*. ed. Dan H.L. *The Bodely Head Bernard Shaw Collected Plays with their Prefaces*. Vol. 2. London: Max Reinhardt, 1980. p. 23.
63. J.L. Wisenthal. *Shaw's Sense of History*. Oxford: Clarendon, 1988. p. 103.
64. *Ibid.*, p. 78.
65. *Ibid.*, p. 38.
66. Stephen Winsten. *Days with Bernard Shaw*. London: Reader's Union, Hutchinson, 1951. p. 235.
67. J.L. Wisenthal. *Shaw's Sense of History*. Oxford: Clarendon, 1988. p. 49.
68. *Ibid.*, p. 47.
69. Shaw. "Preface." *The Good King Charles's Golden Days*. ed. Dan H.L. *The Bodely Head Bernard Shaw Collected Plays with their Prefaces*. Vol. 7. London: Max Reinhardt, 1974. pp. 206-07.
70. J.L. Wisenthal. *Shaw's Sense of History*. Oxford: Clarendon, 1988. p. 77.
71. Interview with Archibald Henderson. "Bernard Shaw Talks of his Saint Joan." p. 45.
72. Shaw. "On Going to the Church." *Non-Dramatic Writings of Bernard Shaw*. ed. Dan H.L. Cambridge: Mass Riverside, Hongton Miffilin, 1965. p. 83.
73. Shaw. "Preface." Plays Pleasant. ed. Dan H.L. *The Bodely Head Bernard Shaw Collected Plays with their Prefaces*. Vol. 1. London: Max Reinhardt, 1971. p. 372.
74. Shaw. "Shaw's Music." ed. Dan H.L. *The Bodely Head Bernard Shaw Collected Plays with their Prefaces*. Vol. 2. London: Max Reinhardt, 1980. p. 230.
75. Shaw. *Our Theatre in the Nineties. A Selection from the Criticism* edited by Hunekar, London, 1932.
76. Shaw. "Farfetched Fables." ed. Dan H.L. *The Bodely Head Bernard Shaw Collected Plays with their Prefaces*. Vol. 7. London: Max Reinhardt, 1974. pp. 427-28.
77. Omar Khayam. "Rubaiyat." Trans. Edward Fitzgerald. G*olden Treasury.* Calcutta: Oxford University, 1997. p. 330.

78. Shaw. "Epistle Dedicatory." *Man and Superman*. ed. Dan H.L. *The Bodely Head Bernard Shaw Collected Plays with their Prefaces*. Vol. 2. London: Max Reinhardt, 1980. p. 519.
79. *Ibid*., p. 493.
80. Shaw. "Man and Superman." ed. Dan H.L. *The Bodely Head Bernard Shaw Collected Plays with their Prefaces*. Vol. 2. London: Max Reinhardt, 1980. p. 531.
81. *Ibid*., p. 572.
82. *Ibid*., p. 573.
83. Alfred Tennyson. *Morte D'Arthur*. Delhi: Aarti Books, 2004. p. 158.
84. Shaw. "Man and Superman." ed. Dan H.L. *The Bodely Head Bernard Shaw Collected Plays with their Prefaces*. Vol. 2. London: Max Reinhardt, 1980. p. 674.
85. *Ibid*., pp. 684-85.
86. Shaw. "Back to Methuselah." ed. Dan H.L. *The Bodely Head Bernard Shaw Collected Plays with their Prefaces*. Vol. 5. London: Max Reinhardt, 1972. p. 430.
87. Quoted by Collins in Raghukul Tilak. *Man and Superman*. Delhi: Rama Brothers, 2005. p. 13.

Chapter 3

Evolutionary Trends in Shaw's Art and Ideas

> It is always so more or less: the novelties of one generation are only the resuscitated fashions of the generation before last.[1]

The genius behind a great work of art, as we can see, lies in its being evolutionary in form, in character and spirit. G.B. Shaw's plays are the tremendous illustrations of the art of this realm. We cannot think of an art ending where it began, it must move all along up and up, following the spirit of evolution, growing and expanding in order to meet the existing contemporary demands of the situation on one hand, and on the other, pointing to the future with its higher objectives and noble aspirations. Looking back at his plays, supported and fired by his revolutionary zeal and attainable objective, analysis and judgment of things, we find Shaw to be justifiably attacking the existing social, political, economic and religious institutions of his times. Naturally, the spirit demanded that a critic and a reformer of Shaw's stature should not stop or be satisfied just by criticizing them as did his Norwegian mentor, Henrik Ibsen. In fact, it was Shaw's higher objective with peerless insight into things, that he took the drama of amusement to the Drama of Purpose to greater heights, in pursuit of providing philosophic as well as practical solutions to the issues concerned. Shaw is nothing if not evolutionary, he can be observed following constant evolutionary trends, all the time connecting the past to the present and extending over to the future thematically as well as technically.

For an evolutionary artist like Shaw, burning with zeal of change and reform, it is the creative urge which becomes so compelling and so forceful as to first correct and reform. It is then on the ashes of the old that he builds and rebuilds and passes the legacies of purpose and hopefulness to future generation. This sense of continuity and flow of values and ideas arise from the sense and urge to be curious, critical and evaluative in order to solve and serve, making the dramatist's art and ideas problem-solving, all embracing and comprehensive instead of merely providing dramatic pleasure and amusement. Shaw's plays are thus found to be truly underlined by an evolutionary trend, so that each one of them can be illustrated as representative of his organized and planned revolutionary mind and thinking. It was to critically analyze and form a new world, not of dreams or of fairy tales, but one based on the impulse to realize certain higher goals, which would pursue the right track to wisdom and real enlightenment, instead certainly of posing "a self-appointed headmaster of the universe"[2] as ironically put by one of his critics.

The secret of Shaw's evolutionary mind and thought can be traced back to the early years of his struggle associated with revolutionary people and their similar doctrines. For this indeed, Shaw had to pick and choose from among the schools of philosophies; the ideas scattered around him. His discerning eyes caught hold of socialist ideas through which he could observe very minutely the ailments of societies, the choice of which changed the whole current of Shaw's life. His new ideas became instrumental in transforming the very current of the contemporary tends in art and philosophy. It was indeed Shaw's selfless love of humanity, and respect for man that by the co-operative efforts of these realistic thinkers, he was able to envisage a better world, the dream of which came through the writings of Samuel Butler that revealed to him the existence of purpose in place of the Darwinian "chance" that helped Shaw trace the purposive Life Force behind the working of the universe. Life Force as perceived by Shaw showed the real place of woman and her ruthless pursuit of the right man and man's intelligent co-operation with the entire scheme. All such efforts would be designed towards hastening the evolution of mankind to higher morals, intellectual, economic, and social orders, rendering drama and the stage as his most suitable medium of expression that could help reform and educate society and institution on purposive lines.

In order to appreciate and perceive Life Force which is the essence of life and its spirit, we will have to do away with all our fictitious imaginings about life and prick the bubbles of fancying the world of things unreal. In fact, Shaw's philosophy of life is so coherent and comprehensive in respect of human nature that what is to come needs to be revolutionary, keeping on the spirit of continuous growth and expansion. For Shaw, the reality behind the world of senses is some extraordinary and urgent pushing and pressing power which is the Life Force. This theory of Life Force is the most dominating evolutionary mark, underlying his plays and can be suitably illustrated through his most recognized masterpieces, namely *Man and Superman* and *Back to Methuselah* series of plays, showing the way to Creative Evolution. Historically, Shaw's philosophy of Life Force draws much of its inspiration and influence from the nineteenth century scientific theories. The biologists believed that in the beginning there was all matter and no life upon the earth but this matter upon the influence of specific and rare physical conditions came to life, gradually and steadily evolving into higher and higher forms, culminating into what came to be known as Erasmus Darwin's famous theory of Natural Selection and "Survival of the fittest" attributing its pattern of evolution to mere "chance". Others like Lamark, assigned it to climactic occurrence in the physical world. All such theories however, were unanimous in denying any working of a divine or spiritual force behind it. It was Samuel Butler who saw the possibility of some living and independent force, showing some scheduled 'purpose' behind the creation. Shaw's Life Force is considerably influenced by this theory which he later recognized and further reoriented into his own philosophy. Life, according to Shaw, exploits matter as a tool. It cannot evolve or develop without entering into matter, creating living organism. Shaw thinks that life has two-fold purposes. Firstly, the immediate purpose is to acquire fresh faculties and higher intelligence. Matter is life's adversity, yet in its adversity it helps life in its efforts towards advancement and acquisition of new powers and new faculties. Dr. Iqbal offers similar views, when he calls the matter as "the whetstone", an instrument upon which life sharpens itself into excellence and power, aspiring into recognition and attainment of the self. Secondly, the ultimate objective of Life Force is not only to depend upon matter but to conquer it in order to evolve further, to shape into a perfect world.

As for the nature of Shaw's Life Force and the way it operates is evidently unlike Thomas Hardy's Immanent Will; a blind and ceaseless striving without any purpose or direction. Shaw's Life Force is purposive, vital and well-directed, with a burning will to create matter and mould it into what was not created. This process of evolution comprises four stages, first "desire", then "imagination" and then "will" followed by "creation". In the beginning of the Back to Methuselah, the serpent explains to Eve:

> ...imagination is the beginning of creation. You imagine what you desire; you will what you imagine; and at last you create what you will.[3]

Shaw's evolution does not merely aspire for greater forms of beauty or physical power, but concentrates on higher forms of intelligence, power of insight and vision as willed by Life Force, through constant process of trial and error. Life for Shaw is something of a divine temper-with a tremendous load of responsibility, which man, alone being God's representative on earth, is obliged to carry out. It is under this pressure that man finds opportunity to develop and sharpen his faculties of intellect, power of observation and his sense of freedom of choice and goodness. It is through this gift of faculty of head and heart that for Shaw, man is able to interpret the meanings and significance and higher objectives of life. Thus, man alone of all the creations can help share in the process of Creative Evolution.

The effort to pursue further is the essential destiny of man, so that the process of Life Force does not stop at any creation point but continue to flow on to generation after generation. This is the handing down the banner or the torch of knowledge and wisdom, to continue life in ceaseless stream with the help and support of human will. Again the Serpent tells Eve, "Death is not an unhappy thing and when you have learnt how to conquer it... By another thing, called birth."[4] This Life Force with its unique power and pressure of purpose and zeal is capable of moving mountains and breaking the magic web of time and space.

Yet again Adam in *Back to Methuselah* feels the monotony of the eternal life of the Garden of Eden. He demands his legacy to be passed on. Adam wishes, "If only there may be an end some day, and yet no end! If only I can be relieved of the horror of having to endure myself forever! If only the care of this terrible garden may pass on to some other gardener!... Only, there must be some end, some end: I am not strong enough to bear eternity."[5]

It is the similar force of human will, like the Life Force, which creates and dominates over the elements that can turn rock into mirror and poison into elixir. "It is again the same transcending power of the life force that to whose emergence and conquest the elements like the sun and the moon look forward in earnest. And to be blessed by the sublimity of his thought and character to share with nature in her creation."[6]

Human life and its related progress subsist in the context of Life Force, moving in ceaseless stream crossing over the boundaries of death in the shape of resurrection. Shaw again conceives Life Force as working through woman to create man who is designed to carry life to higher levels. Nature insists on using the woman to carry on its higher achievements. Shaw on his part mocks at the very romantic notion of love that serves to reduce woman's stature by glorifying it. He erases the assumption, "that the woman must wait, motionless, until she is wooed."[7] Nature fulfils itself through woman's strong determination to carry on the work of Life Force. Eve realizes that, "Creation must not be strangled." She tells the serpent, "I tell you I will create, though I tear myself to pieces in the act."[8] The ruthless pursuit of Ann in *Man and Superman* changes the opinion and the traditional conception of womanhood. Woman has never been a subordinate and a passive receiver, and to remember she was always a strong and determined being. Shaw truly says, "every woman is not Ann; but Ann is Everywoman."[9] She is a part of evolution, moving at a kinetic speed to present before the world the "Superman". This Superman, as envisaged and anticipated by Shaw, is not going to descend from the Heavens; rather he would be a result of the divine gift given to man of striving for the enhancement and excellence of his faculties. He is to be born, bred and nurtured in the world of the matter and hard realities. The idea of procreation is possible through a woman, but if she happens to negate or lack it biologically, then what is to be done? Unfortunately, she is often made to suffer, simply because she can't do so. The concept of womanhood has been attached to that of procreation. Yet, a woman remains a woman by the virtue of her birth and gender rather than her ability to participate in the process of procreation. Shaw's Life Force must be revised here, as it overlooked the crucial role of a woman. She is not always the "ruthless pursuer", who looks up to a man as an agent to help her procreate; she is a human with intellect, feelings and emotions, desiring to share love and care with her life partner in the line of evolution. Any theory that subordinates a woman's position to a man's is far away from the divine base. Man and woman are born equal. The differences lie only in the nature of their responsibilities to be carried on in order to ensure a good life. I propose an intelligent woman's guide to instinct.

Darwin's theory took the world by storm. In spite of its splendid discovery and the undercurrent of Natural Selection and the upper hand of the fittest, goes down in Shaw's estimation because of its being attributed to the result of "chance" rather than a purposive design. Shaw, with his creative insight looks comprehensively and penetratingly into this theory to find its frailty that lies in its being divorced from spirit of religion, in order to achieve a right destination. In regard to Natural Selection, Shaw has to say something that it actually "accounts for nothing in any religious sense." His concern here is due to the fact that "it leaves untouched the whole sphere of will, purpose, design, intention, even consciousness."[10] His definition of religion accumulates what was left by Darwin's theory of Natural Selection. Shaw's interpretation of religion settles the matter. He says, "a religion is nothing but a common view of the nature of will, the purpose of life, the design of organism, and the intention of evolution."[11] His theory of Life Force accommodates these quite well. A true religion gives a framework of sound law and order and thus, it becomes a central aspect of Life Force.

Instead of having just a handful of rituals, with hardly any trace of a bond with the realities of life and the baffling intricacies of human situation, the religion that Shaw seems to recommend is very near to a complete, organized and comprehensive code of conduct covering all departments of thought and action. The concept of evolution as a philosophy, in fact, is the offspring of what Shaw calls "will" which is basically involved in a "mystical process", which can be perceived "only by a trained, apt, and comprehensive thinker."[12] In the light of Shaw's evolutionary scheme of things, religion occupies the central place. Religion is a must for individual as well as for the society. It alone can distinguish between the naive and the wise, the blind and the one with vision and insight, so that the evolutionary product of religion is a great man, who is to be the Shavian hero, combining the matter with the spirit, the ruler with the saint, and the Church with the State.

Nearly a century and a half back, Thomas Carlyle, the celebrated British philosopher-historian observed that, "a great man is ever...possessed with an idea,"[13] the concept of which comes pretty close to Shaw's who is preoccupied with great ideas leading to certain higher missions. The most representative of Shaw's plays presenting and glorifying this "idea" according to critics is *Saint Joan*, which is distinguished as being possessed by a religious idea. Saint Joan, here, does not remain a mere military conqueror, but a strong means towards the fulfillment of a higher religious purpose.

Shaw being a comprehensive philosopher is all the time visualizing characters in the light of history which is composed of a coherent and continuous current of events, connecting past, present and future, into one single unity. This is why his historic hero Julius Caesar, is viewed differently from Shakespeare's Caesar. Shaw's Caesar is to be understood by the modern contemporary group of people whose demand is of a hero who does much more than simply eating, drinking, sleeping and walking on the stage. Caesar is possessed with "idea" and an attainable goal.

The historic split of the church and the State; where the State signifies the ruler and the material world is reflective of the fact that the Church at the time of the split remained incapable of holding and sustaining the State and vice-versa. The restoration of the Church and the State demands restoration of the natural and divine unity of the Church, because then and only then can it hold and sustain the State, not only providing a balance between the two, but emphasizing the grip with the essential pioneering of the Church. However, perhaps the split of the Church and the State owes to reasons, deeper and more subtle, than what is generally attributed to it. In G.B. Shaw's religious context, he clearly disapproves of the trinity and its concept, which I think may have contributed to his severe attack on the so-called corruption of the Church. In Shaw's opinion, it is next to impossible because of the frailty and corruption to which the Church has fallen into like the Salvation Army in *Major Barbara*. He says, "Rather must I point out to it that it has almost as many weaknesses as The Church of England itself."[14] In fact, he finds it in a much deeper state of corruption because, "It is even more dependent than the Church on rich people."[15] Shaw as a socialist rejects capitalism and plutocracy, which are together responsible for upsetting the social, moral, economic order, and the rest of the institutions of society.

The emergence of both capitalism and plutocracy are just the sad results of industrialization in modern times. Poverty "the vilest sin of man and society"[16] is the outcome of capitalist world along with the plutocratic reign. Shaw acknowledges that money is the most important of all human needs, so his Andrew Undershaft preaches money as his religion. This man is created by Shaw in order to express and reveal the ugly side of poverty which is the root cause of all the seven deadly sins. This poverty has been fatal to many civilizations before, Shaw warns, it can destroy our own, if we do not care to concern ourselves with the revolutionary idea by compulsory education. Shaw therefore, builds his socialism on the ashes of capitalism and the extreme side of poverty and plutocracy.

In *Intelligent Woman's Guide to Socialism*, we find Shaw writing that capitalism made England to acquire an empire, "with the curious result, quite unintended by the British people, that the centre of the British empire is now in the East instead of in Great Britain, and out of every hundred of our fellow subjects only eleven are whites, or even Christians."[17] This change from the West to East can be a logical development of capitalism. "And it is no more possible than the transfer of the mighty Roman empire from Rome to Constantinople was possible."[18]

We are reminded of this transfer of Constantine's capital of the Roman Empire from Rome to Constantinople in the fourth century, only to awake the contemporary slumbering lot, erring imagination and false sense of pride. This is Shaw's warning and his "own perception of what had happened in more recent history, could happen in the future."[19] Therefore, mankind must take a responsible stand to adjust "itself to the creative conception of Evolution."[20] In the fifth part of *Back to Methuselah*, the playwright transcends from the presence of time to as far as thought can reach. Here we witness many new cultures with a new and much longer life span of the mortals. She-ancient, a very wise character sharply criticizes Shaw's contemporary as well as our own time perhaps. She tells the Newly Born who cracks from an egg shell that, "There was a time when children were given the world to play with because they promised to improve it. They did not improve it."[21] Shaw here has already minimized the modern standing of the modern civilized world with an optimistic underlying tone to save it from the fall. He is aspiring again for evolutionary development. Another matter of concern lies in plutocracy which is seen as a stumbling block in the process of progress and wider development in all spheres of life, prevalent in Shaw's drama. He asserts:

> Plutocratic inbreeding has produced a weakness of character that is too timid to face the full stringency of thoroughly competitive struggle for existence and too lazy and petty to organize the commonwealth co-operatively.[22]

The question arises as to who is to organize the State? The incapable ruling classes often the richest, consists of the ill-bred rulers or the uneducated masters or educated people who have been badly educated. There is no choice left but to prepare the common masses for taking upon this responsibility of ruling, for which the primary step is to educate them in order to keep them aware and updated. Like all other systems of government, democracy falls in Shaw's estimation. Democracy which unifies Liberty, Equality, and Fraternity, is often manipulated and misused. Shaw in *Apple Cart* is concerned with major economic problem of how to produce and distribute the subsistence, and also with the criterion of selecting the rulers without letting them abuse the authorities in their own interests, also at the same time preventing their class and religion from doing so. There is no other way now but to breed the masses at such a crucial time. Shaw suggests, "We must either breed political capacity or be ruined by Democracy, which was forced on us by the failure of the older alternatives."[23] He suggests the participation of the general masses in the formation of the government, so as to carry forward the civilization towards progress and development. In *Man and Superman*, Shaw draws our attention to the existing social, political and other maladies as well, only with the hope and solution to amend and carry on with the process of evolution which nature in the form of Life Force has bestowed upon humans. The play underlies the assumption that the entire mankind needs to evolve further in order to cope with the problems of civilization. But the littleness of the lesser minds stops progress and growth. In regard to this very matter, Shaw pens down the details as he thought:

> The more ignorant men are, the more convinced are they that their little parish and their little chapel is an apex to which civilization and philosophy has painfully struggled up the pyramid of time from a desert of savagery. Savagery, they think, became barbarism; barbarism became ancient civilization; ancient civilization became Pauline Christianity; Pauline Christianity became Roman Catholicism; Roman Catholicism became the Dark Ages; and the Dark Ages were finally enlightened by Protestant instincts of the English race. The whole process is summed up as Progress with a capital P.[24]

This paragraph offers a forceful and an outright rejection of the Macaulayite concept and faith in progress and the Whig view of history.

Shaw began writing his *Man and Superman* after a span of three years of *Caesar and Cleopatra*, making a firm base of rejecting the theory of progressive historical model. The main assumption that feeds and nourishes in *Man and Superman* is that mankind needs to evolve further in order to meet the demands and the problems of his civilization. We can find in one of the pages in Tanner's *Revolutionist's Handbook* offered by Shaw, entitled *The Verdict of History*, a recapitulation of the arguments we have just been looking at in the *Caesar and Cleopatra* as noted above. It is in response to the proposition that there has been "a progressive moral evolution operating visibly from grandfather to grandson", Shaw through Tanner, the hero, replies:

> ...a thousand years of such evolution would have produced enormous social changes, of which the historical evidence would be overwhelming. But not Macaulay himself, the most confident of Whig meliorists, can produce any such evidence that will bare cross-examination. Compare our conduct and our codes with those mentioned contemporarily in such ancient scriptures and classics as has come down to us, and you will find no jot of ground for the belief that any moral progress whatever has been made in the historic time, in spite of all the romantic attempts of historians to reconstruct the past on that assumption.[25]

This calls to check our modern progress with capital P.

The gone nineteenth and twentieth century, which unfortunately, also can speak for our post-Modern twenty-first century, has a sad story to narrate. Our pride and glory of advancement laughs at our faces, reflecting upon the inner sham and deadly decay. The petty wars of power with the consequence of terrorism seem to be so rampant that not even the new born is spared to hear, see, and feel the impulses of it. Moral progress is out of questions, for our laws are made to ensure utmost security of life to the crime accused, where the victims struggle to survive in a torn condition and ultimately dies. Media profits from the case, same as the law makers do. Here survives just the much hollow talks!

Shaw's anti-progressive approach is quite evident from the very structure of the play *Back to Methuselah*. It is divided into parts and not into Acts. The play comprises five plays within one broad title *Back to Methuselah*, covering history from the Garden of Eden until a period of 30,000 years in the future and as far as thought can reach. The modern period, the time at which the play was written comes only in the second of the five plays. So to believe, that the cycle continues from the Garden of Eden, the very beginning of creation, to the modern era of Shaw's own time. On pondering and speculating, one can come to the conclusion conveying the conviction that there is nothing of any significance that has actually occurred in between. The fall of Adam and Eve from the heavens that took place "In the Beginning" with its foretelling and hinting at future time is constantly felt in "The Gospel of the Brother's Barnabas", which is set shortly after the First World War. Here we see practical side of the theories all over. "Adam's invention of death, and Cain's invention of murder and war are thriving."[26] And Eve's lamentation over her children signifies all mankind to realize the responsibility of life bestowed to mankind. She cries to Cain, "You were a man-child when I bore you. Lua was a woman-child when I bore her. What have you made of yourselves?"[27]

It is our hand in all matters that have been wrongly moulding us, only if we are to realize and mend our ways and reorient our thoughts, progress maybe possible. The argument between Eve and Cain still continues:

> **Eve.** I thought for a moment that perhaps this strong brave son of mine, who could imagine something better, and could desire what he imagined, might also be able to will what he desired until he created it. And all that comes of it is that he wants to be a bear and eat children. Even a bear would not eat a man if it could get honey instead.[28]

Cain is symbolic of modern men of civilization who are busily involved in wars and destruction without any scope for evolution and progress. This can hardly be termed a progressive period of history.

The fourth part of *Back to Methuselah* entitled "Tragedy of an Elderly Gentleman" is set in the year 3000. Its title-character is a survival from previous era in the sense that he is a short-lived, some of his views regarding progress as a responsible citizen of England is thoroughly obsolete. When he encounters a long-lived girl named Zoo on the shore of Thames, he talks of the past and the present in high Macaulayite progressive style:

> I was illustrating-not, I hope, quite infelicitously-the great march of Progress. I was shewing you how, shortlived as we orientals are, mankind gains in stature from generation to generation, from epoch to epoch, from barbarism to civilization, from civilization to perfection.[29]

The two characters continue to argue on longevity of life where Zoo interrupts, "we are made wise not by the recollections of our past, but the responsibilities of our future."[30] She is talking of the steps mankind must take ahead towards evolution, leaving aside the wrongly perceived glorious past and the dogmatic principles of right and wrong. She tells him, "It is not enough to know what is good: you must be able to do it."[31] The Elderly Gentleman tries to close on the topic of discussion. In response to Zoo's emphasis on the importance of longevity, he concludes the discussion by generalizing man and his nature, "Human nature is human nature, longlived or shortlived, and always will be."

> **Zoo.** Then you give up the idea of progress?
>
> **The Elderly Gentleman.** I do nothing of the sort. I stand for progress and for freedom broadening down from precedent to precedent.

Zoo catches hold of his hidden pride and calls him a "true Briton,"[32] who is very much the victim of superiority complex of the Victorian era. In course of the play, the Elderly Gentleman finally gains maturity in thought and understanding of the purpose of life and the higher spirit of Creative Evolution.

Shaw's works are the embodiment of his anti-Victorian bent; they invariably refer to a thoroughly fair and reflective assessment of social values and trends. In Shaw's view, the nineteenth century is not pre-eminently the age of parliamentary democracy, but rather, it is the age of capitalism and plutocracy. The Reform Bill of 1832 regarded as the greatest achievement of nineteenth century England by Macaulay is rejected by Shaw. For Shaw, "it inaugurated the purse-proud reign of the English Middle Class under Queen Victoria."[33] Macaulay considered the nineteenth century as the best of times, but for Shaw, as for Carlyle, Ruskin and William Morris it was the worst of times. The second half of the nineteenth century saw the emergence of Darwinism, which Shaw considered as another sign of perdition, "this Darwinist irreligion persisted into the twentieth century," observes Wisenthal, "and in the second half of Shaw's life he generally included the twentieth century with the nineteenth as the nadir of history."[34] This again entirely rejects Macaulay's concept and theory of progress. Shaw's theory of progress accounts for the Creative Evolution, propagating progressive approach towards development of thoughts, because for Shaw, thinkers are necessary prerequisites for evolution, which can take place only when thought is incarnated in men and women of action. To remember, thought remains impotent when separated from the sphere of action.

Shaw is deeply committed to the idea that there has hardly been any progress in history so far, but he has an equally deep commitment to the possibility of progress in the future. As a responsible dramatist, Shaw views the two sides at once. In the Hell Scene of *Man and Superman,* both the Devil's pessimistic theory of reassurance and Don Juan's optimistic theory of progressive Life Force are equally valid and are compelling ways of looking at the world. This dual perspective in the Hell Scene is again noticed in another form at the beginning of the later play of Shaw in *Buoyant Billions*. Here the son who is ambitious to better the world tells his father that, "At first sight there is no hope for our civilization," but continuing he makes a point that, "At second sight the world has a future that will make its people look back on us as a mob of starving savages."[35] Shaw's bringing together the first sight and the second sight has an importance because there is a ray of hope in finding the defects in the present, so as to correct them, sooner or later, and thus bring about some prospects for the future.

Life force aims at attaining its goal through human race with a tremendous energy that refuses to stop. It tries to improve upon mankind, not merely in tangible shape but intellectually developing the mind so as to carry the civilization toward progress in all the areas of life. But Shaw's idea that evolution if not taken seriously will not necessarily carry mankind up wards, is expressed in a different way in some of his writings, where he warns the people of the world that Life Force may clear the entire human race and replace it probably with a new creation. Goethe has been reported observing in the first half of the eighteen century, "I see the time coming when God will take no more pleasure in the race, and must again proceed to a rejuvenated creation."[36] Goethe was prophesying this possibility for later centuries, whereas Shaw placed this possibility of the end of human existence in the near future. Shaw explicitly expresses this verdict in a lecture on 'Christian Economics,' warning the audience quite politely yet effectively:

> Ladies and gentlemen, it is not an impossible thing that some day or other, there may walk out of a bush somewhere a new being of which you have no conception, not a man at all, or a woman at all; something new that has never occurred before: and the work of God may be handed over to that new thing; and it may be said of us: 'These people have failed; they are scrapped; they are gone.' Part of the mission of the new thing would be to destroy these people as part of the mission of man was to destroy the tiger. Think of that possibility, ladies and gentlemen; and make up your minds to work pretty hard.[37]

This horrid possibility of the ultimate collapse of civilization is not just the downfall of nations but it is the decline and end of human race. The hard work which Shaw is talking about is taking up a responsible stance in order to live and see a better tomorrow. The Serpent tells Eve that, "Adam has invented something new. He has invented tomorrow."[38] Mankind will have to invent new and good values to do the work assigned by nature. The Serpent once again makes us aware that, "As long as you do not know the future you do not know that it will not be happier than the past. That is hope."[39]

It is this hope that inspires human race to live and carry on the job assigned by the Almighty God in the form of Life Force. This hope enables the imagination to conceive the possibility of a better future. *Back to Methuselah* reveals Shaw's dramatic handling of the future in the way that Carlyle, Ruskin and Morris handled the past; as ways and means to bring forth the defects of the present time for good reasons. We can say that in relation to Thomas Carlyle's making of the past and present with that of Shaw's is something new. Carlyle's past and present takes a new shape of Shaw's future and present because Shaw is always for the future. His ideas are marching with evolutionary progress at a bidding speed. Shaw's *Back to Methuselah* can be placed parallel to Milton's *Paradise Lost*, where both the works are about fall of mankind and an ascent. There is again hope of the possibility for improvement depicted bellow:

> If our civilization is facing a crisis in which greater human capacity is required, then perhaps Mankind will rise to the challenge and achieve greater heights; this is what happens in *Back to Methuselah* after the crisis of the First World War, and this is what Juan predicts in the Hell Scene of *Man and Superman*.[40]

We have to hold on to the idea that even if human race is to be swept away, it will definitely be replaced by something new and better. The destruction of human race may be a part of the dual theory of decline or progress depending upon perspective. And Shaw makes us see this part of theory in both the ways with broader perspective. As for Macaulay's rather dogmatic view, idealizing the Victorian England as a glorious period in history, he regards it as mankind's highest achievement so far. But for Shaw it is the making of mankind, the coming up of the super race, which is nature's noblest of the missions and highest achievement so far. This optimistic universal appeal in Shaw's thought and art can be observed as his major contribution, standing the test of contemporary time. It becomes one with Shaw's artistic trend in his art and mighty ideas spread over the two centuries and beyond, and perhaps as far as thought can reach. But for G.B.

Shaw the vision and the mission of the art are not confined to the boundaries of any particular native community. The goal is the creation and coming up of a superior race armed with the genius of a unique character, blending the material and the divine.

Notes

1. Shaw. "The Devil's Disciple." ed. Dan H.L. *The Bodely Head Bernard Shaw Collected Plays with their Prefaces*. Vol. 2. London: Max Reinhardt, 1980. p. 31.
2. As observed by Prof. Father Lauler. Saint Xavier's College. India, 1957.
3. Shaw. "Back to Methuselah." ed. Dan H.L. *The Bodely Head Bernard Shaw Collected Plays with their Prefaces*. Vol. 5. London: Max Reinhardt, 1972. p. 348.
4. *Ibid*., p. 345.
5. *Ibid*., p. 351.
6. Mohammad Iqbal. *Kulliate-Iqbal*. Delhi: Kutub Khana Azizia, 2002.
7. Shaw. "Man and Superman." ed. Dan H.L. *The Bodely Head Bernard Shaw Collected Plays with their Prefaces*. Vol. 2. London: Max Reinhardt, 1980. p. 509.
8. Shaw. "Back to Methuselah." ed. Dan H.L. *The Bodely Head Bernard Shaw Collected Plays with their Prefaces*. Vol. 5. London: Max Reinhardt, 1972. p. 358.
9. Shaw. "Man and Superman." ed. *Dan H.L. The Bodely Head Bernard Shaw Collected Plays with their Prefaces*. Vol. 2. London: Max Reinhardt, 1980. p. 519.
10. *Ibid*., p. 531.
11. *Ibid*., p. 532.
12. Shaw. "Back to Methuselah." ed. Dan H.L. *The Bodely Head Bernard Shaw Collected Plays with their Prefaces*. Vol. 5. London: Max Reinhardt, 1972. p. 297.
13. Carlyle. "Sir Walter Scott." *Critical and Miscellaneous Essays*. iv. 33 works.
14. Shaw. "Major Barbara." ed. Dan H.L. *The Bodely Head Bernard Shaw Collected Plays with their Prefaces*. Vol. 3. London: Max Reinhardt, 1971. p. 40.
15. *Ibid*.
16. *Ibid*., p. 31.
17. Shaw. *The Intelligent Woman's Guide to Socialism, Sovietism, and Facism*. London: Constable, 1949. p. 314.

18. *Ibid.*
19. J.L. Wisenthal. *Shaw's Sense of History*. Oxford: Clarendon, 1988. p. 136.
20. Shaw. "Back to Methuselah." ed. Dan H.L. *The Bodely Head Bernard Shaw Collected Plays with their Prefaces*. Vol. 5. London: Max Reinhardt, 1972. p. 580.
21. *Ibid.*
22. Shaw. "Man and Superman." ed. Dan H.L. *The Bodely Head Bernard Shaw Collected Plays with their Prefaces*. Vol. 2. London: Max Reinhardt, 1980. p. 515.
23. *Ibid.*, pp. 514-15.
24. Shaw. "Caesar and Cleopatra." Act V. ed. Dan H.L. *The Bodely Head Bernard Shaw Collected Plays with their Prefaces*. Vol. 2. London: Max Reinhardt, 1980. pp. 294-97.
25. Shaw. "Man and Superman." ed. Dan H.L. *The Bodely Head Bernard Shaw Collected Plays with their Prefaces*. Vol. 2. London: Max Reinhardt, 1980. p. 773.
26. J.L. Wisenthal. *Shaw's Sense of History*. Oxford: Clarendon, 1988. p. 121.
27. Shaw. "Back to Methuselah." ed. Dan H.L. *The Bodely Head Bernard Shaw Collected Plays with their Prefaces*. Vol. 5. London: Max Reinhardt, 1972. p. 365.
28. *Ibid.*, p. 372.
29. *Ibid.*, p. 517.
30. *Ibid.*, p. 518.
31. *Ibid.*, p. 520.
32. *Ibid.*
33. Shaw. *The Intelligent Woman's Guide to Socialism, Sovietism, and Facism*. London: Constable, 1949. p. 215.
34. J.L. Wisenthal. *Shaw's Sense of History*. Oxford: Clarendon, 1988. p. 100.
35. Shaw. "Buoyant Billions." ed. Dan H.L. *The Bodely Head Bernard Shaw Collected Plays with their Prefaces*. Vol. 7. London: Max Reinhardt, 1974. p. 313.
36. Quoted in J.B. Bury. *The Idea of Progress*. 1920, New York: Dover, 1955. p. 259.
37. Allan Chappelow. "On Christian Economics." *Shaw: 'The Chuker Out.'* London: George Allan and Unwin, 1969.

38. Shaw. "Back to Methuselah." ed. Dan H.L. *The Bodely Head Bernard Shaw Collected Plays with their Prefaces*. Vol. 5. London: Max Reinhardt, 1972. p. 353.
39. *Ibid.*, p. 356.
40. J.L. Wisenthal. *Shaw's Sense of History*. Oxford: Clarendon, 1988. p. 125.

Chapter 4

Contemporary Theatre and G.B. Shaw's Contribution

In order to analyse, evaluate and understand the worth, valuation and the potentials of a work of art or a literary period and the influences and the trends as set and created by it, one is bound to examine the time and the environment of which the concerned artist or the playwright is the by-product. But many a time it so happens that a giant figure of intellect and curiosity among the crowd emerges, who determines his own era. Shaw emerged to make history in the literary world of British theatre combining the two eras on a common platform, with the aim of taking every movement ahead, evolving to carry human civilization towards exploring new horizons and fresh tomorrows. These two eras are the late nineteenth and the early twentieth century, as already focused earlier. Shaw's contemporary nineteenth century witnessed the revival of "both wit and woe in the theatre",[1] and the social problems were being dealt with evolving a new form of drama; the Drama of Ideas having a serious realistic tone where the theatre and the life in town and cities merged. Theatre remained no longer, simply a place for amusement; it opened all the pages of life from the past, present and those in the anticipated future. This brought development of the modern theatre in existence. From 1900 onwards, the modern theatre witnessed the final culmination of stage commercialism with the rise of repertory playhouses inspired by the Abbey Theatre in Dublin in 1903 and the Gaiety Theatre in Manchester in 1907. No time in history before the English theatre had "shown a keen, eager, and informed interest in current dramatic movements outside its own national boundaries."[2] The rapid production of translated works of the great dramatists like Ibsen, Strindberg, Chekhov, Toller and others added to the fortune of the theatres and literary advancement in addition to the exploration of the fundamental dramatic attitudes in Britain. The Two World Wars left their impression on the theatre but literary historians deny any break in the dramatic art and its trend during these two World Wars. If we are to trace the dramatic achievements of the modern period as a whole, we have to look at the general tendencies as well. Establishment of the prose realistic plays is one among such tendencies. These realistic plays are the obvious domain of our dramatist G.B. Shaw, whose concern is to portray critically personal relationships of the characters, along with the presentation of theatrical images of wider social forces borrowed from real life, culminating in particular stress upon 'ideas', often combining the comic and the serious. Whatever may have been the dramatic composition the element of instruction never escaped the literary pens. Hence, the quality of entertainment was subsequently declining. Shaw with his remarkable tools of wit, humour and paradoxes carried forward his theatrical venture to the height and glory of dramatic achievement. He provided Problem Solving Plays to the Problem Plays, turned Comedy of Manners to Comedy of Purpose, all under a broad heading the Drama of Ideas, that could further develop and reach maturity with philosophic idea of Life Force which is "an animating spirit instilled into man with the purpose of energizing him to produce a higher type of creature, the superman."[3] This theory finally culminated into his larger theory of Creative Evolution, "signifying the idea of man-made-perfect through the conscious development of the will-to-be-made-perfect."[4] Shaw's inexhaustible spirit of inquiry accumulates almost all the issues of life in his wide dramatic umbrella that he gave to the world very tactfully and intellectually. At the same time Shaw had to respond to his critics through his powerful argumentative prose composition presented often dramatically and sometimes undramatically through his prefaces. For Shaw, drama is the medium to express and perform all that exists in the air we breathe, the food we take and the actions we make. Tarleton in *Misalliance* rightly expresses:

> There are times when a man needs to meditate in solitude on his destiny. A chord is touched; and he sees the drama of his life as a spectator sees a play.... In the theatre of life everyone may be amused except the actor.[5]

Truly, it is to show this drama of life so minutely to the larger audience by bringing them very close to the psyche of the actor who is seldom amused, with the intention of generalising one set of reality explicitly on the wider stage. So the time to "meditate in solitude" occurs in the theatre itself. There is then no room for pretentions left. There can be no use pretending to close eyes to the obvious, to remain placid where feeling is demanded, to be lost in the world of fantasy when reality has so much to reveal. There is then no room for pretentions left. So true that, "the quicksands make life difficult." But, "still, there they are. It is no use pretending they are rocks."[6] It is no use pretending to call quick sands as rocks. Shaw tried to keep away from idealization of any period of history, literature and people. But his admiration for the medieval era critically sets to examine, scrutinize and make necessary corrections for the sake of bettering and improving his own time and times ahead. Shaw in his essay (1896) for the *Savoy* magazine entitled "On Going to Church", argues that the decay of religious art from the sixteenth century to the nineteenth century was not caused by any atrophy of the artistic faculty, but was an eclipse of religion by science and commerce; that is the aesthetic superiority of the Middle Ages is owing to the medieval world's superiority as a society.[7]

Shaw draws this contrastive picture to take the issues concerned with man and society of his contemporary time to critically study the Victorian and the Modern Age by highlighting the converging and diverging elements from a historical perspective. Every work of art or literature has some value because it is an embodiment of thought and action of that particular time. The reflection of this life enables the generation to form a critical opinion which has to be based on a keen observation and true analysis with a balanced view and discerning judgement. Shaw undertakes to amend and improve upon the shortcomings of his own period with an extended vision and insight, also for many generations to come. Therefore, we find him all the time raising issues concerning society and its institutions with a critical eye and sometimes very strongly commenting upon the British nation culturally as well as morally. He does his best to understand the profound nature and purpose of life which is a succession of events providing lessons at every moving step ahead and thus life must be lived well enough to be properly understood because every passing moment of life is a constant learning experience. It can be seen that Shaw's ideas are always on the forward march of development and evolution so as to keep on the right track of exploration. Shaw believes that there is always some scope for improvement and advancement on the road to evolution, provided we start thinking fairly and deeply over issues without being unrealistic or falling prey to sentiments and to utopian ideas. One may find Shaw's views akin to those of Alexander Pope's whose sense of tradition and ancestry here can provide insistence and emphasis on the force and urgency of evolution and human life:

> We think our fathers fools, so wise we grow;
> Our wiser sons, no doubt will think us so.[8]

Shaw is seen warning his contemporary generation in *Intelligent Woman's Guide to Socialism* "Do not be deceived by modern profession of toleration."[9] It is for the sake of emphasis upon evolution that these two artists deny a sense of superiority of the present over the past. A mere assumption of superiority cannot evolve man's thought and improve his condition. He will have to learn to understand himself and his environment, keeping pace with the velocity of time. Shaw provides us with several Maxims; one of the Maxims for Revolutionists appended to *Man and Superman* is that, "Those who admire modern civilisation usually identify it with steam engine and electric telegraph. Those who understand the steam engine and the electric telegraph spend their lives in trying to replace them with something better."[10] In Shaw's judgement mechanical discoveries and inventions do not mark genuine progress or evolution. Shaw is, indeed, desirous of tracing excellence in the quality of human character, in its area of intellect and morality. The present lack of intellect and decay of values is evident and realized in *Major Barbara* from a modern and advanced perspective.

Andrew Undershaft, in the aforesaid play, complains, that the so-called advanced world is all the time ready to scrap its obsolete steam engines and dynamos and replace them with better and newer ones, "but it wont scrap its old prejudices and its old moralities and its old religions and its old political constitutions. Whats the result? In machinery it does very well; but in morals and religion and politics it is working at a loss that brings it nearer bankruptcy every year."[11] The instances of apparent progress such as the Factory Acts turn out to be, the only changes which money makes, with its false show and momentary effects. In *Man and Superman*, Shaw writes:

> Still, they produce an illusion of bustling progress; and the reading class infers from them that the abuses of the early Victorian period no longer exist except as amusing pages in the novels of Dickens. But the moment we look for reform due to character and not money, to statesmanship and not to interest or mutiny, we are disillusioned.[12]

Therefore, it is only modification in human character that could create the possibility of progress in morality, religion, politics and others. Shaw makes a sharp and factual distinction between mere mechanical improvement and real progress in a long note appended to *Caesar and Cleopatra* on 'Apparent Anachronisms', which is one of the main expressions of his anti-progressive belief. He believes that no progress has taken place since the time of Caesar and Cleopatra. By the popular concept of progress Shaw never means an increased command over the world of nature, but rather an improvement in the world of human faculties of thought, feeling and action. And the common belief with all its celebrations that there has been progress, is the result of "the ordinary citizen's ignorance of the past combined with his idealization of the present."[13]

Shaw's aspiration is to go much beyond the preceding periods in history and to stay ahead of his present time of historical development, by keeping a constant check over the individual and the society collectively. All that was real in life and society of his contemporary time was staged with a forceful effect of ideas and logical debates in theatres of Britain and beyond. The emphasis always remains, even today, on mankind to face the challenges of life and to evolve further to cope with the problems of civilization. Such a drama cannot be to pass away time or to amuse oneself, instead, it provides ways and means to solve the emerging issues and problems of contemporary society. The reason behind Shaw's concern for the Middle Ages is in the use of the period to demonstrate the relative iniquity of his own time of the Victorian and the Modern era. In this context, Shaw and Thomas Carlyle share a common ground. Wisenthal rightly observes that, "Shaw in the tradition of Carlyle, Ruskin and Morris, is drawn to medieval civilization, particularly as an alternative to the debased present." It is also found that England itself shoulders the responsibilities of this "debased present."[14]

In *Everybody's Political What's What?* There is a note of distress with a clear warning that a civilization cannot make any headway on its social, economical, political, religious and educational areas if it is "falling out-of-date." With a particular reference to England in this matter, Shaw says:

> I maintain that in all five we are dangerously behind the times, and will go to the pieces like all former civilizations known to us unless we give our institutions a thorough overhaul pretty frequently.[15]

Back to Methuselah like many of Shaw's plays seeks to shock our normal concept and notion that England is the only important place on the globe with an ideal government. It is to critically view and change perspectives from outside of the scheme of things. It is by careful and logical removing the conventional assumption of England, as having acquired the central place against the inferior peripheries. In *Heartbreak House,* Captain Shotover questions his fellow English people on Shaw's behalf. He asks, "Do you think the laws of God will be suspended in favour of England because you were born in it?"[16] This question highlights the fact that England is just another country, having no special or important position in the world. If we are to examine the shortcomings related to a certain community and its people, we must, like Shaw, take into consideration its social, political, economical, and religious workings, and its consequent results in the form of capitalization, plutocracy, poverty, and various corruptions, all leading to destruction and war. Confucius, a Chinaman in the third part of Back to Methuselah in 'The Thing happened' is involved in an intense argument regarding political, social, economic and other matters. Arguing he tells Burge-Lubin, the President:

> I did not say you could do nothing. You could fight. You could eat. You could drink. Until the twentieth century you could produce children. You could play games. You could work when you were forced to. But you could not govern yourselves.[17]

These remarks only highlight the very basic things a nation or a community is capable of doing. With some deep hidden sentiments, he concludes on England's inability to correctly govern itself. Again and again, Shaw hints that England is lagging behind the time. Confucius, the Chief Secretary to Burge-Lubin, the President, is all the time very critical towards England. He tells Burge-Lubin that, "Your information here is always twenty years out of date."[18] It is important here to note, that this third part of *Back to Methuselah* Shaw prophesied in distant future in the year 2170 AD. Shaw is even apprehensive about the future. Their argument grows so intense that the President's language becomes abusive calling Confucius "You fat yellow lump of conceit!"[19] Englishman's narrow view of personality confines him in the gaiety of appearances. Confucius's reply is here for us to check the insult:

> Only an Englishman could be so ignorant of the nature of government as to suppose that a capable statesman cannot be fat, yellow, and conceited. Many Englishmen are slim, red-nosed, and modest. Put them in my place, and within a year you will be back in the anarchy and chaos of the nineteenth and twentieth centuries.[20]

To live in a fool's paradise is indeed very harmful for the person and also for his environment of which he is a product. It is the matter of concern when Shaw's contemporary nineteenth and twentieth century is said to be in "chaos". Shaw's demand is to evolve in pure thoughts that can come only by giving up "to contemplation," (so that) "great thoughts would come."[21]

Once again, we find Shaw bringing up the subject of the great responsibility, that the nature has entrusted upon human race.

This time it is through the dramatic personae of Mrs. Lustestring who has lived about three hundred years crossing many phases in the history of England. She remarks:

> When I think of the blessings that have been showered on you, and contrast them with the poverty! the humiliations! the anxieties! the heartbreak! the insolence and tyranny that were the daily lot of mankind when I was learning to suffer instead of learning to live! when I see how lightly you take it all! how you quarrel over the crumpled leaves in your beds of roses! how you are so dainty about your work that unless it is made either interesting or delightful to you you leave it to the negresses and Chinamen, I ask myself whether even three hundred years of thought and experience can save you from being suspended by the Power that created you and put you on your trial.[22]

In succession, we find England being incapable of meeting the demands of nature and Life Force. It is considered a prosperous nation which has been negating its values, being unable to manage things very effectively and seriously. A sharp contrastive picture is drawn where the ill consequents of society like "poverty", "humiliation", "anxieties", "heartbreak", "insolence" and "tyranny" are vividly expressed. These ugly consequences are felt because the English have been taking life and its matters like a fun for pleasure. It is significant to note that this instance of satire and criticism is not through a Chinaman or any outsider but by an English woman who has viewed and scrutinized England and its ways from the historical to the distant future in history from within the sphere.

Another significant result of the deterioration was the birth of capitalization. Shaw being a socialist to the core intended to heavily charge against capitalism in many of his works. The economic imbalance was due to accumulation of wealth in few hands. "In the twentieth century the ideal share holders were so rich, as it was called, that they had become the most intellectually lazy and fat headed people on the face of the earth."[23] In the *Intelligent Woman's Guide to Socialism* wrote Shaw, that capitalism caused England to acquire the empire "with the curious result, quite unintended by the British people, that the centre of the British Empire is now in the East instead of in Great Britain, and out of every hundred of our fellow subjects only eleven are whites, or even Christians!"[24]

This shows the graph sliding down where England is losing much that was its pride including its value and religion. "And that this insignificant island is to be retained only as a meteorological station, a bird sanctuary and a place of pilgrimage for American tourists." This sort of condition "or would be a perfectly logical development of Capitalism. And it is no more possible than the transfer of the mighty Roman Empire from Rome to Constantinople was impossible."[25]

Another warning is given by Shaw in *Heartbreak House* which makes us conscious of the things and values that is to be destroyed. Sharing with Carlyle, again Shaw thinks that the French Revolution and the First World War could have been avoided, but it came to be realized through the period of time that they were appropriate punishments for falsehood and incapability of standing to the test of time and reality. Shaw in *Heartbreak House* is not busy warning about the time to come but he very sensibly points towards the punishments that is already seen and felt in the present time of the century.

Shaw in *John Bull's Other Island* makes us aware of the system of government; England has been imposing in commonwealth countries throughout the globe. Adopting the several ways to govern, it has adopted democracy. *The Epistle Dedicatory* to *Man and Superman* has a glimpse of reality on the subject. Shaw accepts that, "Our political experiment of democracy" is indeed "the last refuge of cheap misgovernment."[26] Coming back to *John's Bull Other Island,* Shaw in the preface says:

> It will be observed that no Englishman, without making himself ridiculous, could pretend to be perfectly just or disinterested in English affairs, or would tolerate the proposal to establish the Indian or Irish system in Great Britain. Yet if the justice of Englishmen is sufficient to ensure the welfare of India or Ireland, it ought to suffice equally for England. But the English are wise enough to refuse to trust English justice, themselves, preferring democracy.[27]

Can rules be equal for both the oppressor and the oppressed? Historical survey points to the contrary. Deeply wounded by the atrocities of English colonization and its unjust ways of governance, Shaw's Irish blood warms up and he cannot find any reason to spare the English Nation. He highlights the hidden fact of the English being "wise enough" to be aware of its short comings in the matter of governance and rule by choosing democracy for themselves. Few pages later, in the same preface he contemplates on the fate of his own Ireland, which has been the victim of England's brutal governance itself. "Ireland has been deliberately ruined again and again by England." The reasons are obvious, "unable to compete with us industrially, she has destroyed our industries by the brute force of prohibitive taxation."[28] What happens to the question of Brotherhood and amity between nations to form a coherent whole? The reply maybe very simple, on the way to fulfil a selfish appetite one pulls the other's leg down and in this process itself falls in the pit. So that progress and evolution made may remain very slow. If the world as a whole has to prosper, it must understand the notion that "united we stand and divided we fall." But will the country in question; the Great Britain and its race get cured of their illness of heart and mind? There is but little hope for it to regain its stature and stand unprejudiced with the rest of the world.

Fortunately, Shaw seeks to reconstruct societies through peaceful-intellectual means. He approaches the problems of civilization with easy ways. His reconstruction is also not through wars which are often fought to end wars. Shaw in the preface to the *Geneva* entitled 'An immoral victory' gives a final comment after much discussion on the two World Wars, condemning it to the deepest core. "At every development it is complained that war is no longer justifiable as a test of heroic personal qualities, and demonstrated that it has become too ruinous to be tolerated as an institution."[29]

Democratic setup upsets the system quite intrinsically. Wars have proven to be failures so has democracy. Actual reason behind this philosophy exposes the ill-bred politicians and rulers who being incapable of handling their own little lives and its affairs only end up complicating and corrupting the system with the superficial manners and glittering appearances. Shaw's tracing of real historical-political personae is a fine example in the context here. He writes:

> Even Franklin Roosevelt won his first presidential election more by a photograph of himself in the act of petting a baby than by his political program, which few understood: indeed he only half understood it himself.[30]

On the next page in the same preface, Shaw collectively remarks:

> All the evidence available so far is to the effect that since the dawn of history there has been no change in the natural political capacity of the human species. The comedies of Aristophanes and the Bible are at hand to convince anyone who doubts this. But this does not mean that enlightenment is impossible.[31]

The collapse of "the ancient empires were never destroyed by foreign barbarians," it has always been due to "the work of their own well meaning native barbarians,"[32] who destroyed themselves. Therefore, it is evident that destruction of any civilization has not been through plunders and invasions but has been through the inner decay and delay. The dramatist's business through many such revealing dramatizations is to unveil false appearances in order to get to the reality. It is through "an eminent leadership, experience, and organizing talent" that one can deal with such critical emerging issues. A possibility to attain a fuller life is not through "human attainment but" through "human possibility and hope."[33] At the same time we find Shaw in deep contemplation. He observes:

> How long, then, would it take us to mature into competent rulers of great modern States instead of, as at present, trying vainly to govern empires with the capacity of village headmen.[34]

In this preface to *Geneva*, written much later in Shaw's long span of life, he thinks of his masterpiece that showed and spoke of human life and Creative Evolution with a sure possibility of attaining human improvement and progress. He recollects, "In my Methuselah cycle I put it at three hundred years: a century of childhood and adolescence, a century of administration, and a century of oracular senatorism." In addition to this, he writes, "but nobody can foresee what periods my imaginary senators will represent. The pace of evolutionary development is not constant", but "what is certain is that new faculties, however long they may be dreamt of and desired, come at last suddenly and miraculously like the balancing of the bicyclist, the skater and the acrobat." To end on a happy and hopeful note, "The development of homo sapiens into a competent political animal may occur in the same way."[35]

And once this side of man develops there can be no stopping of evolution. This may be universally applied to mankind in general. Shaw's mission to show the mirror to the world is not only to reveal the defects in various ways but to provide remedy to the human race both in the past and present extending to the far reaching future, and as far as thought can reach. This is all said and done by an effective means chosen by Shaw through dramatic presentation covering the period of the two mighty eras of nineteen and twentieth century.

As for Ireland's contribution to the world of drama, it has evidently been immense. The Irish National Theatre, at Abbey Theatre in Dublin, opened up new opportunities for new dramatists. Important names associated here with drama are J.M. Synge (1871-1909), Sean O' Casey (1884-1964) and Lady Gregory (1852-1932). For nearly ten years, William Butler Yeats (1865-1939) made an effort to bring into life the Irish National Theatre, and then began a radiant period of Irish drama. However, W.B. Yeats's contribution has mainly been more poetic than dramatic, though he also produced some notable poetic plays like *The Land of Heart's Desire* and *The Countless Cathleen*. It was Yeats who motivated Lady Gregory to the theatre, where apart from organising and managing, she gave some uncommonly well-observed little plays of her contemporary modern Irish life and character in *Seven Short Plays* (1909) and few others. It seems the artists were busy observing facts of life and their works reflect their surrounding situations and people. Sean O' Casey is celebrated for two of his plays concerning contemporary town life in Ireland, *Juno and the Paycock* and *The Plough and the Stars*. J.M. Synge put his dramatic writing to a different comic style in his masterpiece of twentieth-century theatre, *The Playboy of the Western World*. His cynical comedy was a mixture of realism and fantasy with thoughts of death kept alongside scenes of hilarious merriment. Such a comedy along with Lady Gregory's related plays like *Spreading the News* and others may not have a direct association with the current plays of English stage, but indirectly they helped in the growth of comedy in British theatre. The British stage during twentieth century was marked by historical events and epoch making achievement leading to scientific trends culminating in the two World Wars that left lives altered, shocked, and disrupted. But this did not disturb the dramatic development; instead it led to the rise of psychological conflicts and realism in theatre.

John Galsworthy during this period established himself as a dramatic force with a new school of social drama in the play *The Silver Box* in 1906. He tried to give social drama a tragic form and effect, where social structure and situations gained prominence and theatrical effect, in place of characters. Galsworthy fell short of suitable prose medium to meet the demands of the tragic form in drama. He was unable to discover suitable words to express and convey his intended message through dialogue as well as stage directions. In short, Galsworthy failed to successfully respond to the urgent artistic call and dramatic demands of the time.

Bernard Shaw's attention and hold on his contemporary generation emerged from the prominence of his plays as commentaries upon contemporary affairs and issues connected with real life situations. As time passed, his influence began to be felt in the works of other artists of Britain and other countries of the world, establishing Shaw for posterity due to his unquenchable optimism and hope in man's ability and ultimate preparedness in the form of Life Force and Creative Evolution to bring forth the Superman.

Moving further from Shaw's immediate contemporaries in drama we come across some figures, who like Ibsen and Shaw changed theatre. An important name among a few is that of Samuel Beckett (1906-89) another Irishman. But before moving to next generation of dramatists we must look through the attitude and dramatic form of August Strindberg's (1849-1912) dramaturgy. It was in Shaw's time when Nietzsche was in vogue, that Karl Marx, Erasmus Darwin, and Freud in their own ways were challenging the established laws of universe which till then had been thought unchallengeable. Here, old beliefs crumbled and new were at the reach, where every truth depended on perspective, emerged Strindberg, who unlike other playwrights expressed his own ideas through new set of dramatic personae. His characters were "lost, confused, frightened, irrational."[36] They were spiritually unsettled, self-questioning and self-divided, with unlocked passions. Guided by unknown vaguely sensed disturbing forces, their talks in the form of dialogue naturally shifted and changed erratically and sometimes quite ill-logically. Strindberg's *Miss Julie* reflects the very spirit of its own time both in content and form. Dramatist of this tragic play acquired colour in his style through anger, courage and urge to know people's secret realities. Unlike Ibsen and Shaw, who were supporters of women's emancipation, Strindberg subjected his women characters to the "same ruthless and sceptical observation, which had, long been accepted in the creation of male characters."[37] Strindberg failed to give solutions to the problems making an intense tragedy from social ground. It was his peculiar approach to unravel concrete truth to wider range of people and society. Though not intended to change society, but definitely with an aim to make them aware of their ill surroundings and this can still be set to bring revolution in thought and behaviour of mankind.

It is often seen that controversy ignites interest, so did Samuel Beckett's controversial play with unconventional script *Waiting for Godot* in 1953. This phase of twentieth century was diving deep to search for some unique dramatic genre, in a sense it was gathering from the sparks left by its predecessor's to evolve into a new set of drama called Drama of Absurd. Shaw had already changed the traditional notion and deliverance of drama, which was earlier to tell a story, often of conflict that was to become the basis for the play's action and revelation of character. Actions in his plays were replaced by logical arguments and fiery debates. Further, Beckett discarded the idea of any action and even arguments, to focus inaction as his main trend introducing a new genre, Theatre of Absurd. Such a play would exhilarate the playgoers by its presentation. "Beckett was eliciting a surprisingly deep and complex response from the often crazy juxtaposition of word, gesture and silence."[38] Everything that happened on stage had specific images and was both clear and mysterious at the same time. *Waiting for Godot* focuses in the first words of the play, "nothing to be done." Beckett cleverly makes his audience and the characters in *Godot* wait for something to happen in the play and in their lives too. It has no plot and a rather static situation, but the two tramps Estragen (Gogo) and Vladimir (Didi) wait anxiously for the arrival of unknown person named Godot. Beckett himself in an interview declared on being questioned "Who is Godot?" replied, "If I knew, I would have said so in the play,"[39] leaving it a philosophical puzzle. The play makes the silence as important as dialogue "not only the kind of silence that comes to all of us in everyday life, or the silence of characters in their anguish, but a peculiarly Beckettian silence, the presence of an absence that is palpable, touching the heart of existence, as if in the beginning was the silence, then came the word, then the silence again."[40]

Godot removes the most important part of realistic theatre; the character recognition, and without being connected to any history, any naturalistic background, it gains universality. A simple juxtaposition of comedy and tragedy makes the genre as uncertain as everything else in the play. Beckett first wrote this play in French and later himself translated it into English language with a subtitle 'tragicomedy,' because like Shaw he distrusted classification, and stopped his critics from emphasizing the comedy over tragedy or vice versa. Perhaps those who are true artists and critics of life like Shaw and Beckett are seekers of truth. They hesitate from making classifications because it is unnatural, for reality mingles everything. In *Godot*, with balances of both silences and emptiness, Beckett caught the mood of his time. Amid the cloud of present day's centerlessness, purposelessness and godless air, Beckett waits for some kind of salvation. Much like Shaw was waiting for Superman, Beckett is seen, yet, anticipating in hope because unlike Shaw he was not aware of the person he was waiting for.

Coming closer to our own times in the legacy of Shaw we can observe a rapid growing consciousness and a sense of involvement of the thinker-dramatist to solve the mysteries of life. Artistic pieces from Shakespeare to Shaw and to his contemporaries and to the time of John Osborne, Eugene O'Niell, Edward Albee and Arthur Miller, have observed and portrayed contemporary scenarios in their own ways deepening our responses to dramatic senses and leaving it open for further interpretation. James John Osborne (1929-94) was an English playwright, screenwriter, actor and critic of the establishment. The success of his play *Look Back in Anger* in 1956 upholds the Drama of Idea that once again transformed English theatre. Osborne, in his productive life of more than forty years, explored many themes and genres of our contemporary post-modern time. Like Shaw, Osborne questioned the point of the monarchy on a prominent public stage. Osborne's choice of the Drama of Ideas was instrumental in making him the first among men of letters of his contemporary age to address Britain's purpose in the post-imperial age. *Look Back in Anger* reflects the attitude the time was passing through. The playwright and his dramatic personae are popular even today by the phrase "angry young man." In order to fulfil the current demands, Osborne offered the dramatization of the slice of life on the world stage. This play is autobiographical, and based on Osborne's time living and arguing with Pamela Lane (his wife) in a cramped accommodation in Derby. It comes to our notice on sensible observation and speculation that Osborne was influenced by both Ibsen and Shaw. The commonness among the three playwright's basics of dramaturgy lies in the fact that their plays are modern in outlook and acceptable in real life situations with a clear note of revolt. In the new plays offered by them, the drama often arises through the conflict of unsettled ideas which is not between clear right and wrong. What then makes their plays interesting is discussions, refining and clarifying the issues? We do remember that discussion is of the key importance in Shaw's drama, particularly. Most of his protagonists are polished debaters, but the wit they show is not the Oscar Wilde's epigrammatic wit, but rather the best expression of their own convictions. Coming back to Osborne, his *Look Back in Anger* with all the inhabitants of the play together transformed the British theatre, following a progressive approach. The theatre was artistically made respected again by revolutionizing; changing the formal constrains of the past and present generation by turning the attention once more to the language in use, theatrical rhetoric and emotional intensity. Kenneth Tyan in *The Oserver*, being the most influential critic of the time praised *Look Back in Anger*. He called the play the best young play of its own decade. John Osborne, thus remains a promising dramatist, whose authenticity and originality would no doubt remain an exception. Osborne recognized the theatre as a means to impart his message to the ordinary common people who would collect the courage to break down barriers that have been hampering growth and development of man and society. Osborne, it seems wanted his plays to be a reminder of real pleasures and real pains, drawing sensitivity to the connections between mind and heart, body and soul. The evolution here continues in art and literature with Osborne, whose work brought a difference to the world of theatre, deeply influencing other playwrights such as Edward Albee and Mike Leigh and perhaps would many more in the time coming.

If we are to study Bernard Shaw in the light of a comparative study, we find his ideas matching all periods of historical time to our present twenty-first century, mostly because his works rightly depict human nature which forms continuity, coordinating the present with the past and the future. This comparative and contrastive study can help prove Shaw's evolutionary step.

Shaw's aspiration is to go much beyond the preceding periods in history and to stay ahead of his present time of historical development, by keeping a constant check over the individual and the society collectively. All that was real in life and society of his contemporary time was staged with a forceful effect of ideas and logical debates in theatres of Britain and beyond. The emphasis always remains on mankind to face the challenges of life and to evolve further to cope with the problems of civilization. Undoubtedly, such a drama cannot be to pass away time or to assume oneself alone, it thus becomes a way and means to solve the rising issues and problems of contemporary society. As The Bishop in *Getting Married* says on behalf of Shaw that, "All progress means war with society."[41] Realistic presentation on stage along with naturalism has been an important feature of all revolutionary drama whether it is Ibsen's, Strindberg's, Beckett's or Shaw's. Each of these important playwrights and some before them like Synge, Yeats and Galsworthy created their very distinctive genres adding to the richness and variety in dramaturgy. We also find some dramatists like John Osborn, Eugene O' Neil, Edward Albee and Arthur Miller. Each of these dramatists contributed to the service and promotion of art and philosophy, enriching the art of drama which is undoubtedly, a function of unifying human experiences. With the passage of time, it is assumed that this form of art (drama) assimilates and homogenizes the entire population of the world for a single cause, that is, to work for general masses out of selfless love of humanity. In this global context of creative service, Indian contribution to drama has been immense. We can roughly begin with Tagore (1861-41) and continue to mention a few important names of dramatists in particular of our own time, such as Vijay Tendulkar (1928-2008), Girish Karnad (1938-), Gurcharan Das (1943-), Asif Currimbhoy (1928-) and Mahesh Dattani (1958-).

A discussion of a few among these eminent playwrights can expose their convergence of idea and understanding of the purpose behind the creative urge as an artist, in special relation to Shaw's broader understanding and fuller world view. Rabindranath Tagore is a legendary figure who combined his wide perspective of the nature of things in his artistic faculty. Ideas are vital for artistic creation and Tagore imbedded the same. The foundation of his perspective was education which he enforced upon India to acquire in order to achieve independence from the British foreign rule. He believed that independence from British rule in India itself would be meaningless and merely lead to replacement of a foreign oppressor with natives as long as Indians remained entangled in ignorance, ritualism, superstition, and obsolete ideas. There has been a demand for a better change, by questioning the established norms, and those perceived prides of glories that did not follow the nation towards evolution. This stemmed from

Tagore's opposition to the concept of nationalism as opposed to Gandhian concept of pride and culture chauvinism which led to untold suffering in the first half of the twentieth century both in Asia and in Europe. In addition to this was Mahatma Gandhi's use of religion and a call to revive a simpler pastoral lifestyle, which were to Tagore, a major retrograde step because Tagore favoured a more open, secular, and international outlook. He was quite worried about the wrong direction of some out-worn philosophy, which would stagnate India, if it were to be followed. His theoretical pieces never escaped the powerful force of his ideas. Tagore's drama is rich in variety of themes, with intricate subplots and extended monologues. *Dak Ghar* and *Visarjan* are some notable plays, having subtle suggestive and symbolic approach. His plays, perhaps, are closer to Shaw's. They are less in action, and more in intensity of feeling and thought.

Vijay Tendulkar seems to share a common platform with Bernard Shaw, for his plays derive inspiration from real life incidents and social upheavals, providing clear light to the covered harsh realities. Apart from being a playwright, Tendulkar's vocation was that of a literary essayist, political journalist, and social commentator primarily in Marathi language. He is best known for his plays, *Santata! Court Chalu Aahe*, *Ghasiram Kotwal*, and *Sakharam Binder*, all aspiring to give native theatre a new form. The techniques used in early one act plays connect him to his contemporary European and American writers. Tendulkar's remarkable perception of both the beauty and nobility of the world as well as the ugly and ignoble side of it is like Shaw's use of paradox which is commonly used to explicitly express the nature of human will. With the necessity of portraying tenderness and realism in character depiction, his drama enriched the entire Indian theatre by picturizing the varied problems of native life in Maharashtrian state to generalize the issues and problems on a wider arena. The aim of great minds often merges regardless of their distinct time, space and language, so have been Shaw's and Tendulkar's. The sum of all their efforts was to convey a message through the means of art and literature with the intention of will and purpose to improve man and society and to make earth a better place to live in.

The explosion of people's alienation from contemporary social, moral, economic, religious, and political institution hamper the significant and unavoidable relation between the individual and society. Man's struggle for survival, the varied moralities of living, and their social positions are binding concern, to expose the artificiality of society for good reasons in the form of reform and progress. Thus, we find art serving life, crossing boundaries of time and space. And such art by nature of its own become didactic, emphasizing the importance of making better thoughts, better homes, better family and better society.

Girish Karnad, another playwright of repute has been found to be influenced by Ibsen and Shaw. Karnad borrows his plots from mythology and in the process of his dramaturgy, he treats them with his own style and modernity, connecting them to the contemporary scenario. His *Hayavadana* is inspired both by Sanskrit *Kathasaritasagar* and Thomas Maan's *Transposed Heads*. Karnad dramatises the story through the principle characters, Devadutta, Kapila, and Padmini to show the human urge for the union of the flesh and the intellect, spirit and the matter. On looking at the play's theme, we sense the similarity that lies between Shaw and Karnad, as Shaw is always in search for the completeness in individual and society, hoping to bring the Superman, Karnad looks for perfection and completeness in the very same way. There is dichotomy between the intellect and the body, but in order to meet challenges and bring reform, both are equally required. Shaw and Karnad, though miles and times apart, desired to change society and better human thoughts. Their art remains art for the sake of life.

Quantity in the absence of quality of vision and insight cannot make a man, a great artist. Shaw's loads of dramatic achievements index at the fact that he has a message to deliver, some challenges to meet, and a vision to fulfil. These factors link him with the noted Indian playwright, writing in English, Mahesh Dattani, who is important to this endeavour because "Dattani is an authentic contemporary voice whose plays are routed in contemporary urban experience."[42] He has the unique capacity to read the rumblings of contemporary urban Indian society and smell of perennial clash between tradition and modernity. Dattani's works like *Where There is a Will* and *Tara* show his acquaintance with the works of Tennessee Williams, Arthur Miller and Strindberg. In his dramatic technique, he can be compared to Ibsen in the sense that the ghosts of the past, the dark secrets of human consciousness that torment the present, are explored in a subtle and convincing manner in his plays. In spite of rejecting any attempt to impart any moral lessons to humanity, his works draw our attention to the complex prejudices of our class, gender, race and religion. Shaw's plays also expose the violence of our private thoughts and hypocrisy of our public morals like Dattani's, but their treatment of the subject matter remains apart. Patriarchal concerns are disturbing thoughts even today, though much has been done to improve upon the mindset of people. In *Tara*, Dattani reveals the seamier side of society where females continue to be viewed subjugated and marginalised through the actions of males and also by females. Women being victimised by their own gender is more tragic than otherwise. Equality of gender and liberation of women from the confinement of thoughts call for Shaw's Life Force, which can perform as a common platform for both men and women on equal terms. Their participation remains the hope for betterment of societies and nations, globalizing the larger motive behind the creations. Theatre for Dattani like Shaw is a reflection of observance of things. But to do more than exposition of the real life observance for Dattani is didactic. It can be observed that by simply holding up a mirror is not enough; Dattani does not seem to provide solutions to the problems leaving a heavy load of effort to the audience. What then does it mean to be a playwright? We find him replying to this question:

> I see myself as a craftsman and not as a writer. To me being a playwright is about seeing myself as a part of the process of production. I write plays for the sheer pleasure of communicating through this dynamic medium.[43]

So it seems that Dattani's plays do not aim at changing society through dramatic medium but seeks to offer some scope for reflection in the hope that his drama will give the audience some kind of understanding into their very own lives. While Shaw, on the other hand, broke the tradition of mere exposing some disturbing realities of life. Going beyond, he had the courage to offer solution to the existing and arising problems of man and society through long debates and effective arguments, all heading towards evolution, progress and growth of human will. If we are to ponder and deeply speculate the canvas of Dattani, it can be revealed to us that, even the simple exposition of life-related issues can be problem solving psychologically. In our contemporary scenario, Dattani rightly does what Shaw did in his own time.

On looking at the time before and after the pioneering Shaw, one can draw the conclusion that the indebtedness of contemporary playwrights to Bernard Shaw is indisputable, and undoubtedly that Shaw will be the abiding influence on dramatists for many more centuries to come, he would be confronted if not imitated.

In the realm of drama, William Shakespeare is most often considered a touchstone. Perhaps because Shakespeare's mighty dramatic lines fit into the basics of human conditions in all ages. It is a matter of immense interest to experience Shakespeare, the greatest dramatist of all centuries in multiple forms, and find Shaw's approach to Shakespeare so rich and varied that there can be no escape but to discover their shared insight and vision. Critics opine that after Shakespeare it is Bernard Shaw among those who could really share the rich legacy of British drama to its zenith and glory. In fact, both these dramatists were serving the world through their tremendous art and ideas by holding the mirror to their respective societies in their own individualistic fashion. Shakespeare's dramatic composition is the poetic form, whereas Shaw followed a pattern of prose style in his drama.

As for Shakespeare, he is beyond doubt a great poet-dramatist, but which of the two features is greater and which of the two sustain the other? Shakespeare is basically known to be a dramatist, that is to say, he has mastery over the art of drama and dramatization. But he is equally a great dramatic poet, implying that he enjoyed complete mastery and skill in the art of dramatic poetry, composed strictly to suit the dramatic art and dramatic situations. In this way, although Shakespeare is termed a Romantic dramatist, so his dramatic poetry is different from great romantic poets like Wordsworth, Shelley or Keats or even Byron. Shaw on the other hand, is a prose dramatist. His prose being dramatic prose, very well matches his dramatic art in his own context of the Drama of Ideas and Purpose. He differs from Shakespeare in his approach. Shaw therefore, remains anti-romantic at the base. Yet the two artists can be said to have a common meeting ground, both are great artists exploiting their own respective arts, producing great works of art and masterpieces. Both have something to say, something to give to their audience in the form of message, idea, and a certain philosophy of life, jewelled with a profound sense of beauty, superb enough to engage the readers and audiences spellbound. Some important views in regard to Shakespearean poetic drama include T.S. Eliot's Introduction to the Wilson Knight's *The Wheel of Fire*. He observes:

> The writer of poetic drama is not merely a man skilled in two arts and skilful to weave them in together; he is not a writer who can decorate a play with poetic language and meter. His task is different from that of the "dramatist" or that of the "poet", for his pattern is more complex and more dimensional.[44]

On this "complex" and "more dimensional pattern" Shakespeare successfully carries the dual burden, by fulfilling the demands of both poetry and drama. One among thousand such verses from *King Lear* could be sighted to prove his unmatched competency in his art:

> You do me wrong to take me out o' the grave:
> Thou art a soul in bliss; but I am bound
> Upon a wheel of fire, that mine own tears
> Do scald like molten lead.[45]

Shakespeare was busy portraying characters, reflecting on life's situations, having tremendous appeal because of his superb artistry and his philosophical insight into human nature and character. "The greatest poetry, like greatest prose, has a doubleness", the poet talks on "two planes at once" and Shakespeare had "this doubleness of speech."[46] Although Shaw never wrote poetry, he carried some secret longings for blank verse somewhere sometimes. We find him expressing his admiration for blank verse and its origin, in these lines. "I am quite sure that anyone who is to recover the charm of blank verse must go back frankly to its beginnings, and start a literary, pre-Raphaelite Brotherhood."[47]

Shaw's inclination for blank verse takes us back to his unending desire to revive and relieve the pre-Raphaelite Brotherhood of medieval era. Shaw perhaps could have been a poet-dramatist like Shakespeare as he thinks was easier for him. He admits in the preface, "...the only grammar I ever learned was Latin grammar, so that the Elizabethan English became a mother tongue to me."[48] In the same preface, Shaw writes on loss of the Latin, exerting that, "...with the advent of compulsory education sixty years ago, and the creation thereby of a class which could read and write, but had no Latin and less Greek, newspapers and plays alike soon came to be written by illiterate masters of the vernacular."[49] In a mournful tone Shaw adds, "...and I myself welcomed the change and discarded my early classical style for a vernacular one."[50]

Shaw makes it very difficult for us to decide whether it was his natural style as a prose writer or his only choice. He is but only sorry for the loss of "Latinity," "by the end of the nineteenth century" from "the press and theatre."[51] In the context of Shaw's desire to regain blank verse or his adherence to contemporary dramatic prose that remains unique and remarkable in style and structure, Shaw had always at the back of his mind a suitable and apt means to express his idea and convey his message to his contemporaries as well as posterities.

Sometimes thematically, we find Shaw sharing some common views with that of Shakespeare's. The Shakespearean theme on woman pursuing man is evident in his *Man and Superman*. "In Shakespeare's plays the woman takes the initiative," writes Shaw. Continuing he illustrates further:

> In his problem plays and his popular plays alike the love interest is the interest of seeing the woman hunt the man down. She may do it by charming him, like Rosalind, or by Stratagem, like Mariana; but in every case the relation

> between the woman and the man is the same: she is the pursuer and contriver, he the pursued and disposed of.[52]

Woman a hunter and man a prey is not any invention of Shakespeare and Shaw, rather it is observed as the natural urge in a woman to take initiatives which has found its expression through centuries in the well-intended works of high literature. Thus, converging and also diverging of ideas can always be found in likeminded thinkers and men of letters. It is important to note, that in spite of Shaw's reverence for William Shakespeare, Shaw could not confine his art to the limitations of Shakespeare, as he thought it to be, for which he provided suitable corrections.

Shaw criticized *Othello* on the basis of its romanticism, as opposed to the "actual humanity", for which it becomes a cold-blooded murder and a piercing tragedy. Othello's jealousy and Desdemona's meekness, woven in a romantic assumption is something Shaw cannot tolerate, for "nothing in the theatre is a staler than the situation of husband, wife, and lover, or the fun of knockabout farce."[53] Shaw's *How He Lied to Her Husband* is a very fine comedy made out of the situation mentioned above. In Shaw's own words, we can note the reason he applied to alter the normal nature of things. He says:

> I have taken both, and got an original play out of them, as anybody else can if only he will look about him for his material instead of plagiarizing Othello and the thousand plays that have proceeded on Othello's romantic assumptions and false point of honour.[54]

Shaw is far from emulating. His pen always finds alternative treatment of subject matters. Making comedy out of tragedy of Othellian type is the matter of un-daunting courage, highlighting the developed technical faculty of the dramatist. Shakespeare's dramatization of Julius Caesar in *Antony and Cleopatra* again causes some discomfort to Shaw. Shaw's *Caesar and Cleopatra* alters the case and we find him aiming at historical justice. Annoyingly, he writes, "It cost Shakespear no pang to write Caesar down for the merely technical purpose of writing Brutus up."[55]

Shakespeare portrays human characters with inner conflict of their own particular identity in them. In spite of all praises for Shakespeare's dramatic art, Shaw points out, "but Shakespeare, who knew human weakness so well, never knew human strength of the Caesarian type. His Caesar is an admitted failure: his Lear is a masterpiece."[56] It is not enough to show the weaker side of men and women, rather it is equally important to present the intellectual soundness of personality. Shaw was indeed fortunate to catch the opportunity to improve upon Shakespeare's Cymbeline. In the preface to the play, he pens down:

> The practice of improving Shakespear's plays, more especially in the matter of supplying them with what are called happy endings, is an old established one which has always been accepted without protest by British audiences.[57]

An attempt to improve upon Shakespeare's plays goes beyond an ordinary courage. Shaw manipulated the last act of the play and tried to connect the entire play to his own time. He has carefully "cut out surprises that no longer surprise anybody."[58] The temptations to meddle with master-pieces of an established dramatist, for the "circumstances which demand it"[59] are truly "irresistible" for Shaw. In the context of Shakespearean interpretation, we agree on T.S. Eliot's verdict that concerns an entire set and sum of Shakespeare's drama:

> The work of Shakespeare is like life itself something to be lived through. If we lived it completely we should need no interpretation; but on our plane of appearances our interpretations themselves are a part of our living.[60]

Shakespeare's drama comprises and accumulates a wide range of people and their contemporary issues as its subject matter, which is "something to be lived through." The interpretation thereby becomes necessary to gain proper understanding of the works, which Shaw very well could sense the urgent need for the same. Having understood Shakespeare's nature of work and the tempo of his own age, Bernard Shaw in the year 1949, when having reached the ripeness of his age and having attained wide recognition of his art, was asked to write down a puppet play characterizing Shakespeare and himself. Shaw decided to write the play under the title *Shakes verses Shav*, which resulted in an apparent comedy with a series of physical and verbal battle between the two great dramatists of their respective ages. It is interesting to note Shaw's notion and deep awareness of his own popularity. To Shakes's call he replies:

> **Shav:** Nay, who art thou, that knowest not these features
> Pictured throughout the globe? Who should I be
> But G. B. S.?[61]

The competition in a form of a dialogue begins when Shakes catches Shav, "Laughest thou at theyself? Pullst thou my leg?"

And Shav replies revealing his characteristic critical vein,

> "There is more fun in
> heaven and earth Sweet William,
> Than is dreamt of in your philosophy."[62]

Is Shaw not a philosopher? He definitely is. Here he is only trying to impose his own power of craft, observation and reality, staging attainable dreams. Shaw's and Shakespeare's contribution made to the world of literary drama is in question here:

> **Shakes:** Where is thy Hamlet? Couldst thou write King Lear?
> **Shav:** Aye, with his daughters all complete. Coulds thou
> Have written Heartbreak House? Behold my Lear.[63]

Shaw proudly tells Shakespeare:

> You were not the first
> To sing of broken hearts. I was the first
> That taught your faithless Timons to mend them.[64]

This humourous battle of words excites our imagination. The implication here refers to the significance and status of Shaw as a problem-solving dramatist who worked to provide right solutions and remedies to the problems with abject optimism to the world through his dramatic art. Having achieved success and glory Shaw asks Shakespeare to bear, "For a moment suffer/ My glimmering light to shine."[65] At last, Shaw feels victorious, for his art is for life sake and is problem solving in contemporary set-up and forever more, with long-lasting effect. Before this play begins, Shaw educates his readers, "that Shakespear was not an illiterate clown but a well read grammar-schooled son in a family of good middle-class standing, cultured enough to be habitual playgoers and private entertainers of the players."[66]

Nonetheless, his deep sense of respect for Shakespeare is obvious. He remarks that, "Nothing can extinguish my interest in Shakespeare."[67] In the preface to *The Devil's Disciple*, we find Shaw explaining:

> It does not follow, however, that the right to criticize Shakespear involves the power of writing better plays. And in fact—do not be surprised at my modesty—I do not profess to write better plays. The writing of practicable stage plays does not present an infinite scope to human talent.[68]

In other place, we also find Shaw explicitly warning critics and interpreters in Shakespearean context, that it is not the "craft of the playwright" that changes but only "philosophy" and "the outlook of life" undergo alterations. He replies to those for holding his criticism against Shakespeare, "as blasphemies against a hitherto unquestioned Perfection and Infallibility."[69] Shaw writes, "I have merely repeated in the dialect of my own time and in the light of its philosophy what they said in the dialect and light of theirs."[70] Thus, he meets his targeted goal.

Shaw did realize upon his stature as a dramatist and truly so he was invariably cautious of the feeling that he could rub shoulders with Shakespeare. Shaw is observed to be constantly aspiring to go beyond Shakespeare and perhaps have fulfilled Shakespeare's unaccomplished missions here and there.

Shakespeare's dramatic poetry has the romantic air built up with the purpose to suit his comedy and tragedy, and deals with portraying the intricacies of human nature in a matchless, charming, and unique way, all his own. Shaw's dramatic art may be said to match with Shakespeare's dramatic poetry or at least can be said to come closer to it in terms of effect and influence upon the existing contemporary dramatic trends as well as the future times. Shaw's dramatic prose is meant to suit the temper of his own drama, the Drama of Ideas, written to correct and reform existing institutions through analysis and evaluation, not only to dramatize or entertain. The art of drama is not merely the art of mimicking, or imitating a person, and personage, or portraying situations and characters. It, in fact, flourishes or is meant to flourish in conveying a message through situations dramatically. So, what is significant in the art of dramatization is involving a sense of wonder, surprise, and excitement, in the context of that particular idea or message. Shaw does them all, but differently through his anti-romantic and realistic approach and style. Shaw's contribution to the world of drama is that he lent it a sense of continuity and streamlined it into a process of evolution and progress, coordinating the previous dramatic works and trends to those of his times, thereby stretching the realm of his contemporary drama, making it much wider and richer in acceptance and popularity.

Notes

1. Allardyce Nicoll. *British Drama.* New Delhi: Doaba House, 2005. p. 200.
2. *Ibid.*, p. 249.
3. W.H. Hudson. *An Outline History of English Literature.* Delhi: A.I.T.B.S., 2007. p. 277.
4. *Ibid.*
5. Shaw. "Misalliance." ed. Dan H.L. *The Bodely Head Bernard Shaw Collected Plays with their Prefaces.* Vol. 4. London: Max Reinhardt, 1972. p. 173.
6. *Ibid.*
7. Shaw. "On Going to the Church." *Non-Dramatic Writings of Bernard Shaw.* ed. Dan H.L. Cambridge: Mass Riverside, Hongton Miffilin, 1965. p. 383.
8. Alexander Pope. *An Essay on Criticism.* London: Lewis 1711. Lines 438-39.
9. Shaw. *The Intelligent Woman's Guide to Socialism, Sovietism, and Facism.* London: Constable, 1949. p. 369.
10. Shaw. "Man and Superman." ed. Dan H.L. *The Bodely Head Bernard Shaw Collected Plays with their Prefaces.* Vol. 2. London: Max Reinhardt, 1980. p. 794.
11. Shaw. "Major Barbara." ed. Dan H.L. *The Bodely Head Bernard Shaw Collected Plays with their Prefaces.* Vol. 3. London: Max Reinhardt, 1971. p. 171.

12. Shaw. "Revolutionist's Handbook." *Man and Superman*. ed. Dan H.L. *The Bodely Head Bernard Shaw Collected Plays with their Prefaces*. Vol. 2. London: Max Reinhardt, 1980. p. 765.
13. J.L. Wisenthal. *Shaw's Sense of History*. Oxford: Clarendon, 1988. p. 119.
14. *Ibid.*, 81.
15. Shaw. *Everybody's Political What's What*. London, 1986. p. 344.
16. Shaw. "Heartbreak House." ed. Dan H.L. *The Bodely Head Bernard Shaw Collected Plays with their Prefaces*. Vol. 5. London: Max Reinhardt, 1972. p. 177.
17. Shaw. "Back to Methuselah." ed. Dan H.L. *The Bodely Head Bernard Shaw Collected Plays with their Prefaces*. Vol. 5. London: Max Reinhardt, 1972. pp. 445-46.
18. *Ibid.*, p. 444.
19. *Ibid.*, p. 446.
20. *Ibid.*
21. *Ibid.*, p. 448.
22. *Ibid.*, p. 476.
23. *Ibid.*, p. 477.
24. Shaw. *The Intelligent Woman's Guide to Socialism, Sovietism, and Facism*. London: Constable, 1949. p. 313-14.
25. *Ibid.*
26. Shaw. "Man and Superman." ed. Dan H.L. *The Bodely Head Bernard Shaw Collected Plays with their Prefaces*. Vol. 2. London: Max Reinhardt, 1980. p. 512.
27. Shaw. "John Bull's Other Island." ed. Dan H.L. *The Bodely Head Bernard Shaw Collected Plays with their Prefaces*. Vol. 2. London: Max Reinhardt, 1980. p. 833.
28. *Ibid.*
29. Shaw. "Preface to Geneva." ed. Dan H.L. *The Bodely Head Bernard Shaw Collected Plays with their Prefaces*. Vol. 7. London: Max Reinhardt, 1974. p. 24.
30. *Ibid.*, pp. 26-27.
31. *Ibid.*, p. 28.
32. *Ibid.*
33. *Ibid.*, p. 41.
34. *Ibid.*, p. 42.
35. *Ibid.*

36. Helen Cooper. "Introduction." *Miss Julie*. London: Methuen, 2000. p. ix.
37. *Ibid.*
38. Normand Berlin. "Traffic of Our Stage: Why Waiting for Godot?" *The Massachusetts Review*. Amerest. Autun, 1999. p. 3.
39. *Ibid.*
40. *Ibid.*, p. 5.
41. Shaw. "Getting Married." ed. Dan H.L. *The Bodely Head Bernard Shaw Collected Plays with their Prefaces*. Vol. 3. London: Max Reinhardt, 1971. p. 582.
42. Madhujain. *India Today*. 15 October 1994.
43. Anita Nair. *Mahesh Dhattani: The Invisible Observer*. 8 December 09. p. 2.
44. G. Wilson Night. "Introduction." *The Wheel of Fire: Interpretation of Shakespearean Tragedy*. T.S. Eliot. London: Methuen, 1978. p. xv.
45. William Shakespeare. King Lear. ed. G.K. Hunter (1972-96). *New Penguin Shakespeare*. Lines iv-vii.
46. G. Wilson Night. "Introduction." *The Wheel of Fire: Interpretation of Shakespearean Tragedy*. T.S. Eliot. London: Methuen, 1978. p. xv.
47. Shaw. "The Admirable Bashville." ed. Dan H.L. *The Bodely Head Bernard Shaw Collected Plays with their Prefaces*. Vol. 2. London: Max Reinhardt, 1980. p. 433.
48. *Ibid.*, p. 437.
49. *Ibid.*, p. 435.
50. *Ibid.*
51. *Ibid.*
52. Shaw. "Epistle Dedicatory." *Man and Superman*. ed. Dan H.L. *The Bodely Head Bernard Shaw Collected Plays with their Prefaces*. Vol. 2. London: Max Reinhardt, 1980. p. 506.
53. Shaw. "How He Lied to Her Husband." ed. Dan H.L. *The Bodely Head Bernard Shaw Collected Plays with their Prefaces*. Vol. 2. London: Max Reinhardt, 1980. p. 1031.
54. *Ibid.*
55. Shaw. "Preface." *The Devil's Disciple*. ed. Dan H.L. *The Bodely Head Bernard Shaw Collected Plays with their Prefaces*. Vol. 2. London: Max Reinhardt, 1980. p. 39.
56. *Ibid.*
57. Shaw. "Cymbeline Refinished." ed. Dan H.L. *The Bodely Head Bernard Shaw Collected Plays with their Prefaces*. Vol. 7. London: Max Reinhardt, 1974. p. 179.

58. *Ibid.*, p. 182.
59. *Ibid.*, p. 183.
60. G. Wilson Night. "Introduction." *The Wheel of Fire: Interpretation of Shakespearean Tragedy*. T.S. Eliot. London: Methuen, 1978. p. xx.
61. Shaw. "Shakes verses Shav." ed. Dan H.L. *The Bodely Head Bernard Shaw Collected Plays with their Prefaces*. Vol. 7. London: Max Reinhardt, 1974. p. 473.
62. *Ibid.*, p. 475.
63. *Ibid.*, p. 476.
64. *Ibid.*
65. *Ibid.*, p. 477.
66. *Ibid.*, p. 470.
67. *Ibid.*
68. Shaw. "The Devil's Disciple." ed. Dan H.L. *The Bodely Head Bernard Shaw Collected Plays with their Prefaces*. Vol. 2. London: Max Reinhardt, 1980. p. 41.
69. *Ibid.*, p. 40.
70. *Ibid.*

Chapter 5

Conclusion

Evidently enough, G.B. Shaw revolutionized the stage by breaking the web of confinement and adherence to the generally followed strategies of dramatization. Instead of drawing upon the specific set of genres, he joined the pieces to form the integrated whole in his plays and prefaces. This art came to him only by observing, speculating, and pondering upon nature. He was a shrewd observer of political, social, economic, religious and cultural conventions. In each of these, he found an endless source of artistic inspiration. He is always filled with a bag full of fresh and new springing ideas, and so much so that these were perhaps never said before. In the following interrogative lines, we can reason out the motivating factor behind his facile pen. He himself pens down, "What is the use of writing plays or painting frescoes if you have nothing more to say or show that was said and shewn by Shakespear, Micheal Angelo, and Raphael?"[1] He has been busy, giving the world and contributing much more than anybody else. The lines below accepts the fact that nature has been producing its agents to carry on its message. Therefore, in the words of Shaw, "As a matter of easily observable fact, every generation produces men of extraordinary special faculty, artistic, mathematical, and linguistic, who for lack of new ideas, or indeed of any ideas worth mentioning, achieve no distinction outside music halls and class rooms, although they can do things easily that the great epoch did clumsily or not at all."[2] These are indeed no mere words of support or incentive to the playgoers. However, necessity being the mother of inventions and discoveries, Shaw with his eagle eyes could see the need for corrections in all the spheres of life in the Victorian as well as Modern England. His presence was felt deeply, for he was turning the flow of a new stream towards common life of man and woman, showing the importance of ideas and revolting thoughts. It is observed that Shaw never cared for effective assertion. In his words, we can trace the same thought. "Effectiveness of assertion is the Alpha and Omega of style. He who has nothing to assert has no style and can have none: he who has something to assert will go as far as in power of style as its momentousness and his conviction will carry him."[3] He also objects to the blind adherence of technical development in writing any work of art. We find him arguing in his own typical humorous style:

> If technical faculty were the secret of greatness in art, Swinburne would be greater than Browning and Bryon rolled into one, Stevenson greater than Scott or Dickens, Mendelssohn than Wagner, Maclise than Madox Brown. Besides, new ideas make their technique as water makes its channel; and the technician without ideas is as useless as the canal constructor without water, though he may do very skillfully what the Mississippi does very rudely.[4]

The importance lies in what the writers have to say. Accepting his incalculable position, Shaw says, "But the humblest author, and much more a rather arrogant one like myself, may profess to have something to say by this time that neither Homer nor Shakespear said."[5] This acknowledges the technique Shaw has been using because; whatever he said is said very well. The scenes, his dialogues, and his prefaces direct our attention for speculation and study. The art of description of his scenes gives absolute realistic touches. They have Shaw's minute observation, accurate description of things, time and place, and all the time sticking to realistic portrayal of the same. His scenic details serve to enhance the required dramatic effect pertaining to his theme of the particular play. For example, in *Man and Superman*, in the beginning of the play, Shaw describes, "How old is Roebuck? The question is important on the threshold of a drama of ideas; for under such circumstances everything depends on whether his adolescence belonged to the sixties or to the eighties."[6] Another example describing Mr. Robinson (Octavious) highlights Shaw's remarkable and elegant style of both narration and description, which is very suggestive of the play that, "...all announce the man who will love and suffer later on."[7] The question is if we take away the scenic details, will it affect his proposed dramatic effect of the play? Perhaps yes, because, although superficially unique and unprecedented and rather innovative, each word of it is indicative of providing support; artistic and realistic support to the theme and also to the play itself. Although just imaginary and concord they give their impression of reality, the logically acceptable and believable background and also the context of what is going to take place in the drama. The force and effect of his ideas incorporate the force and strength of his dialogues, which is the indirect conveyance of his messages through characters in his plays. Shaw has used his characters as mouthpieces and spokesmen. His dialogues and discussions also take the involvement of human nature. Therefore, he makes them speak on his behalf, at the same time retaining their specific individuality. His drama forms a wide range of dramatic personae taking inspiration from every sphere of life and institution. His dialogues are more appealing and they re-enforce what the dramatist has to say in his prefaces. After all, prefaces are his direct conveyance of the message, therefore, the dialogues have a greater appeal because discussions and dialogues are more natural, situational, and life like with logical conclusions.

Shaw's prefaces along with his scenic descriptions are deeply integrated with the very concept of Problem Plays and Play of Ideas. The very decision to write prefaces before the real drama, accounts for Shaw's unique courage of conviction, which springs from the force and strength of his ideas, and the style of his assertion, because the dramatist cannot dare sermonize the modern theatre audience without taking the risk of theatre getting deserted, which is a direct refusal to what the dramatist is going to say. This speaks of his rock like self-assurance and firm belief in the validity and force of his ideas. Therefore, there is hardly any gap between what he says and what he practices.

Critics and interpreters tend to associate wit and humor as an integral part of the typical Shavian drama. In fact, if we look deeply and carefully into the texture and the framework of his drama, wit and humor remain with Shaw until late, when he entered the philosophical boundary of his dramatic reflections. It continued to serve him not only to amuse but to provide sugar coatings to the bitter pills he had to prescribe and in the process, as his art progressed, it became one with his style and philosophy. Undoubtedly, during this period he remained a vehement critic and an explorer of various social, moral, and economic maladies, rejecting and eliminating much that had hardly any relevance to mankind and evolution. Until the historical and philosophical plays, his employment of wit and humor worked as an essential device, a must for a proper response and solution. However, plays like *Man and Superman*, *Saint Joan*, and *Back to Methuselah*, seem to be announcing a surer voice and a height of flight and vision. In these plays, we find maturation and full ripening of Shaw's philosophical ideas that were ready to substitute for wit and humor technique. This makes the Victorian melodrama and the associated techniques finally to be replaced by the powerful Drama of Ideas, so deeply and directly touching the literary world around with a much wider range than before. It is as though Shaw's protagonist finding the theatre small and narrow responded to the call of a larger, freer, and wider arena of dramatic presentation. William Shakespeare through his superb tragedies like *Othello*, *Macbeth*, and *Hamlet*, and Shaw in his *Man and Superman*, *Saint Joan*, and *Back to Methuselah* achieved success despite the lurking gap of the various eras of the serious and the comic in making of dramatic history.

Shaw's remarkable prose carries the burden of his philosophy and ideas through staging the various issues and aspects of life and society. But even before we begin reading the play, we are made to encounter an elaborated discussion in the form of prefaces. Shaw as an established preface writer acknowledges his stance in the preface to *The Devil's Disciple*:

> I am ashamed neither of my work nor of the way it is done. I like explaining its merits to the huge majority who dont know good work from bad. It does them good; and it does me good, curing me of nervousness, laziness, and snobbishness. I write prefaces as Dryden did, and treatises

> as Wagner, because I *can*; and I would give half a dozen of Shakespear's plays for one of the prefaces he ought to have written. I leave the delicacies of retirement to those who are gentlemen first and literary workmen afterwards. The cart and trumpet for me.[8]

Such a strength and power of writing prefaces are fully exhibited. It indeed does everyone good. Perhaps Shaw accomplished to fulfill Shakespeare's unattainable goal of preface writing. This workmanship is to be celebrated, but only before passing through a test that any preface writer ought to go through.

A preface is likely to face some challenges, of which, the first among many is the fear of adverse response from the readers, and impending fear of opposing remarks from critics. All these apprehend poor sale and affect popularity. It sometimes may result in affecting reader's motivation to read or watch the play. Writing prefaces become a challenge to the writer himself, to his interpretive and explaining capacity for the positive delivery of the message. It remains a challenge to the writer's intellectual caliber, his critical faculty and to the soundness of his philosophy upon which he bases his theme. And lastly, it is a test to the flexibility and engaging power of his prose style, so elegantly supplementing and enriching his dramatic effect. Shaw remarkably undergoes these tough tests to be classified and declared as a unique preface writer. His prefaces are masterpieces, for they account for the dramatist's ability and tireless courage to accommodate his oceanic ideas. So then his prose style beautifully elaborates all that and even more, in prefaces, that are written for dramatic purpose. Everything energetically emphasizes upon the fact that Shaw wrote prefaces because he was able to, and moreover, these prefaces also become his weapon to suitably censure his critics and interpreters. A critic himself, Shaw evaluated the received criticism on his works quite differently. Having a right sense of humor, his rebukes and scolding to his critics are always digestible and interesting. His attacks are like his prescriptions for social and other maladies which are often sugar quoted. This definitely disturbs the critics. Shaw himself questions his natural habit, "Why did Nature curse me with this fatal gift of driving critics out of their senses?"[9] In his preface to *The Devil's Disciple*, he argues the playwright's common causes; the incapability and fear of writing prefaces. He elaborates and explains:

> The reason most playwrights do not publish their plays with prefaces is that they cannot write them, the business of intellectually conscious philosopher and skilled critic being no necessary part of their craft. Naturally, making a virtue of their incapacity, they either repudiate prefaces as shameful, or else, with a modest air, request some popular critic to supply one, as much as to say, Were I to tell the truth almost myself I must needs seem vainglorious: were I to tell less than the truth I should do it myself an injustice and deceive my readers.[10]

The above-noted declaration can very well-establish Shaw's ability as an "intellectually conscious philosopher" armed with sharp critical faculty that is required for the "craft". It also stands as a fine example for the retort to the critics and interpreters. Preface writing demands skill and intellect from the writers to explain and elaborate the ideas they present that uphold their dramatic presentation. Necessarily, an honest artist and forceful writer alone can do justice to his theme and his objectives. Shaw writes, "I do not think the critics have criticized *Caesar and Cleopatra* worth a cent. I could have done it better myself."[11] It annoys him to find incompetent critics and playwrights attempting to criticize his, historical play *Caesar and Cleopatra*, the literary historical knowledge often kept absent, leaving a void in literary world. Shaw declares it disgraceful for any critic to be ignorant of history, especially those who complained his Caesar and Cleopatra plot to be "ill constructed, rambling, inconclusive and so forth."[12] The answer he gave to this was "as if I had made Roman history".[13] Leaving no part and space uncovered from his debate and discussion of any topic, Shaw wins over the literary world making himself explicitly clear to the readers and audiences around. At the same time he leaves a serious note of warning to the critics, he said, "Yet we must get an electorate of capable critics or collapse as Rome and Egypt collapsed."[14] His warning is to save civilization from the fall because critics, especially those dedicated ones have always been and will continue to be an essential part of the literary world. His prefaces, thus, can be termed as one of the most marked and integrated features of his evolutionary trend in the context of both art and ideas.

With Shaw emerged a new era of revolt and rebellion against both the old fashion of "art for art's sake", and the traditional theatrical norms. This Drama of Ideas through Shaw's voice of rebellion was received by many critics as a betrayal on the part of a "true artist" and his "art". While others like Dickinson thought that even if Shaw is to be termed a dramatist, the stage or theatre does not seem to be his dedicated concern. We can moreover judge the nature and concept of the Shavian drama through Shaw's famous recorded speech that he delivered to the Royal Academy of Dramatic Art in 1928. He said:

> Now what the drama can do, and what it actually does is to take this unmeaning, haphazard show of life, that means nothing to you, and arrange it in an intelligible order, and arrange it in such a way as to make you think very much more deeply about it than you ever dreamed of thinking about actual incidents that come to your knowledge. That is drama, and that is a very important public service to render.[15]

He tried to make people ponder and speculate rather deeply on just-passing events of real life through his dramatic presentations, which are responsible tasks and a high mission for any man of letters and playwright in particular.

The word 'drama' originated from Greek 'drana' that is to 'do', 'act'. In fact, it was meant to emotionalize or sentimentalize through suspense, action and happening of certain events. This area belongs to one of the oldest arts in the history of art and literature. It gained an entirely fresh new looks in the hands of Shaw like in the hands of the alchemist whose job is turning baser metals into gold. The traditional drama confined itself to mimicry and imitation with the help of using emotions and sentiments, just to amuse the playgoers. Shaw looks much beyond, drama being not only his choice but a necessity and urgency with which to put art to its more serious role of sharing with realities of life. This calls for certain unique courage and conviction, which makes art something transcending and connecting to real life situation, rendering art and philosophy, something they had ever been able to attain.

Shaw's conviction about his own individualistic and thoroughly unique understanding and perception of the art of drama, of portraying his ideas and objectives is intensively powerful and revolutionary like P.B. Shelley's the 'Westerly Wind' which serves destroyer as well as preserver. He is therefore, less concerned with failure or success. This is because he is fully aware and convinced of the stream and unflagging effect of the inner and unseen strength of what he calls Life Force, the spirit of which is all pervading, connecting, and exploiting all the worthwhile legacies of the past, present, and also the future. The other integral part of Shaw's Drama of Ideas is its seriousness of motive and intensity of feeling, which in the context of his novel presentation was perhaps to shock and surprise in order to emphasize and seek a favorable response from his play-goers as also of critics. Shaw asserts, "when my books will either perish, or, if the world is still poor enough to want them, will have to stand, with Bunyan's, by quite amorphous qualities of temper and energy."[16] What Shaw means here is the extension of his own realistic philosophical attitude traceable in almost every masterpiece of world literature. His journey is like Bunyan's Christian who makes a pilgrimage and progress that Shaw cherishes to make. This takes Shaw beyond the boundaries of art and philosophy to whose subordination, Shaw is insistent upon throughout his dramatic career. He acknowledges:

> No doubt I must recognize, as even the Ancient Mariner did, that I must tell my story entertainingly if I am to hold the wedding guest spellbound in spite of the siren sounds of the loud basson. But "for art's sake" alone I would not face the toil of writing a single sentence.[17]

Thus, in order to match his lofty address with the audience's expected response, Shaw is seen to be employing all his wonderful dramatic techniques of wit and humor, and paradoxes to sugar coat his bitter pills, but of course, not "for art's sake alone." We find critics often complaining of the lack of emotional strains and sentimental touches in his plays. The answer is obvious. It is in the sense that, social, moral and economic problems look more to intellect and impartial keen observation based on unerring judgment than just emotionalizing the concerned issues. So, the result is the emergence of a powerful means of Shaw's favourite debate and discussion through which he wins his mandate. In place of the "will" along with the clash of destiny, found time and again in Marlowe's and Shakespeare's plays, Shaw is involved in the clash and conflict of ideas. *Candida*, *Arms and the Man* and others are representative illustrations of Shaw's anti-romantic, anti-sentimental attitude and practice, so that those countable emotional passages are brief and rare in his plays. He is mocking at the romantic attitude in the scenes, where Raina expresses her emotions to Sergius. In *Candida*, Marchbank, a poet and a romantic dreamer feels deserted when Candida brings home to him the serious purpose behind the reality of life. Shaw's Saint Joan, while facing martyrdom remains quiet and composed, evidently signifying the dramatist's master stroke and expert handling of subjugating emotions to intellect and artistic enjoyment to philosophic purposiveness.

Shaw's consistent preoccupation with ideas, his consequent social criticism with the purpose, has considerably influenced and channelized his art and technique of dramatization as well as the form of his plays into a unique process of universal communication. In the earlier well-made play prior to the time of Ibsen and Shaw, the first act was devoted to exposition, there was development of situation in the next act and finally we could witness the unraveling in the last act. But Shaw under the terrific pressure and compelling force of the urge of his critical and creative bend, found no way but to alter the very order of dramatization, its spirit and form. So, there is nothing like natural organized plot with a conventional storytelling resulting in characters as personified abstractions.

As has already been traced and asserted that the Drama of Ideas came to Shaw partly as a legacy from his Norwegian dramatist, Henrik Ibsen, and he further expanded and enriched it to make it Problem-Solving. In fact, his Drama of Ideas bases itself on the tools of arguments (having coupled) with the weapons of perception, which is found exceedingly effective towards converting and convincing the human community. To obtain the required effects, Shaw the techniques by his practices to put in use the directness of assertion, and resourcefulness in illustrations. And with his grip over the use of metaphor and simile, all combined with marshalling facts and ordering arguments, with his famous device of paradox, that could shock and surprise the audience with his sarcasm and irony, joined with his all the time ready and brilliant wit and humor to attract and sustain attention and effect.

Here the problem arises as the modern concept of art and literature derives inspiration from the fact that it must amuse, provide interest, and at best reflect by portraying life and its institutions as they appear to be. Further, that those pioneers of this traditional concept of art have always tended to ignore reality behind the appearance, trying to undermine it, so the individual as also his community, psychologically speaking do not remain bound by the otherwise natural instinct of drawing inspiration from the life; its spirit. Such a view of art flourishes in the instinct and outright refusal and rejection of any interference of ideas and values into the realm of art. Henry Arthur Jones is one of the many modern contemporary critics of Drama of Ideas who has always made it his mission to guard against any interference of instruction or values indicating a thoughtful reform and to question such moves encroaching upon the pens of the artists and playwrights. Shaw has the character to revolt against all such departmentalization that serves to split and divide life into zones, which often remains blind to issues concerning mankind and civilization. Joining the tirade against the Drama of Ideas along with some concerned playwright, Arthur Jones remarks:

> With earnest convictions, with consencientious hopes for the uplift alike of the drama and the human race, with eager purposes that are all bound up with the "influence of the theatre upon the evolution of our civilization," with all these admirable aims the playwrights of England and America are "doing nothing."[18]

In fact, art and literature, if not evolutionary, remain cut off from the ups and downs and the main stream of life; they cannot serve its real purpose. Shaw's mission remains to alter things exactly on this line. It is very essential that the artist comes to visualize the larger purpose behind creation, to have coherent and comprehensive view of human nature so as to captivate the ultimate reality behind the world of senses and try to look under the issues of life with an aim of settling them, as well as supporting such aspiring forces to reform and reconstruct culture and civilization. The burden of such a revolution or transformation must be undertaken by the artist and his art following Dr. Iqbal's similar view on the concept of art, as essencially dynamic and serviceable, "be it the poet's voice or the musician's symphony." We find Shaw insisting upon the matter here:

> But ordinary men cannot produce really impressive art-works. Those who can are men of genius: that is, men selected by Nature to carry on the work of building up an intellectual consciousness of her own instinctive purpose.[19]

This change of pattern was to unveil the crude realities often cloaked in necessity of appearances. The intention behind this dramatic move was to involve the common masses in general participation of reading and viewing realities of which they were often involved, but were sometimes afraid to realize and come out for discussion, the reasons being a false sense of honour and pretence. Shaw was to shatter the falseness of the domestic doctrines. *In Getting Married,* he writes, "I could fill a hundred pages with the tale of our imbecilities and still leave much untold."[20]

Such a revolutionary move came as a shock to societies of ladies and gentlemen and much more to the acceptance of it as they denied calling such staging and presentation as drama. But to a resolute philosopher and a skilled artist like Shaw, his critical comments as a playwright were not an acceptance of defeat. For him, it rather became something of a challenge to inspire and thus, spread his message very often with continuous writing and staging of more revolutionary plays, along with his thrashing prefaces. In regard to his *Misalliance*, we can quote Shaw's sharp and judicious comment:

> Well, I wanted to find out whether the critics could really tell the difference between a farce and a tragedy, or a melodrama and a high comedy, unless the author told them. I found they couldn't. 'Misalliance' was a specially

> developed example of high comedy, observing the strictest conditions as to unity of time and place. And the poor critics went about bleating that it was not a play, but only a conversation. They will presently discover that Beethoven's 'Eroica' is not a symphony, but only a musical score. They really are blazing duffers. They walk into my traps every time.[21]

Shaw's sole aim was to convey his thoughtful message in dramatic forms to humanity at large of which he himself was an important part. A genuine artist like Shaw, therefore, found no way but to pursue an evolutionary trend in his art and ideas with certain and definite higher goals that could be effective and problem solving to suit the objectives. The art and artifice are just tools; instruments towards evaluating, diagnosing and settling the various issues of human life and society, so that they could become one with the message, meeting the various required demands and challenges. Shaw commences his dramatic journey with the determination to deal with the real problems of life and society. For this reason he makes a sharp distinction between realism and idealism, focusing the clash between the two, with realism taking an upper hand over idealism, sentimentalism, romanticism and capitalism.

In the preface to *Misalliance*, he explains his concept of imagination very clearly in the suitable context of the English man's behaviours. He says that "the Englishman is wholly at the mercy of his imagination, having no sense of reality to check it."[22] Elaborating the point, he writes:

> Before we can clearly understand how baleful is this condition of intimidation in which we live, it is necessary to clear up the confusion made by our use of the word imagination to denote two very different powers of mind. One is the power to imagine things as they are not: this I call the romantic imagination. The other is the power to imagine things as they are without actually sensing them; and this I will call the realistic imagination.[23]

Historical presentation in remarkable dramatic structure is also a typical Shavian illustration of his art. Though Shaw sees a visible distinction between the two epochs he saw and lived in, he discovers continuity in the nature of human experiences tracing a bond between historical periods. "I require whole populations and historical epochs to engage my interest seriously,"[24] explained Shaw to Ellen Terry in 1897. His embarkment as a dramatist with entire population and distinct periods of history is richly illustrative of his sense of historical approach to the past, present, and the future. His major historical plays like *Saint Joan*, *Caesar and Cleopatra*, and *In Good King Charles's Golden Days* depict Shaw's historical attitudes. They remain informative and instructive enough to alter responses of public and critics alike. A careful study of these works in the light of his historical thinking highlights his inquisitiveness in historical design. Shaw's attitude towards history is quite a part of his Victorian literary environment, as well as, the modern awareness. His understanding of thought and action can be seen through his appreciation of history:

> The truth is that without a sense of human history, life as we know, it would be unthinkable, history being, a fundamental to our lives at that. It is only through a knowledge of history that our own brief lives such a short span of experience becomes one with the record of human race, it is through history that we can know anything of the record and we can share it. The life of the individual breaks its barriers and becomes continuous with humanity.[25]

Remembering that Shaw was a dramatist and not a historian, the one hardly left with choices, we find him rather aiming to attain historical justice through his plays, often adding necessary correction as he thought were needed. Of what he was doing as a dramatist with certain historical characters and situations, enhances our awareness towards making of historical epochs. Bernard Shaw, through long, fertile and progressive journey of his life, discovers later in his historical plays that, "the great man is a person who incarnates an idea, so his conception of a historical epoch is a period of time that embodies an idea."[26] However, the changes have always been needed for progress and evolution. Historical changes occur, when thought is embodied in men and women of action, like Saint Joan and Julius Caesar. But thought when inactive and detached from the sphere of action remains impotent. Thought, the pre-eminent, is the preparatory condition for any historical change. Often we find Shaw offering alternatives and corrections to the past. In this process, he never forgets to compare and contrast the past with the present, revealing again the same shortcomings of his contemporary civilization, and at the very same time of critical evaluation, he surely offers correctives to his own time. His profound concern for humanity is reflective here in historical drama, perhaps written only for the sake of saving man from fall again. It is interesting to note the new sides of historical characters which can hardly be found in historical records. His King Charles is a better man than found in the pages of history, his Caesar is old and tired of the explorations, his Cleopatra is not the admired queen of the mighty Egypt. She is rather timid and afraid in the process. Among these, Shaw justifies his distinct presentation of Caesar. He says, "it seems to me that the very first consideration that must occur to any English dramatic expert in this connection is that Caesar was not Antony."[27] We must ponder here for historical truth, similar to any other kind of truth that is not necessarily a matter of fact. It is, in fact, the question of interpretation and which is nothing but imagination.

In spite of critic's revolt against the presence of edification in any literary piece, Shaw realised that social influences upon literary style can be identified most surely in the didactic works, precisely targeted for edification of people in general. "EDUCATE OR GOVERN," wrote John Ruskin, "they are one in the same word." In the following lines, we clearly see the positive effects of educating the masses through effective means:

> During the sixty-four years of Victoria's reign, a time of hazardous transition, education in England supplemented parliamentary action as a substitute for revolution, for achieving national change without catastrophic violence. The instruction of the masses, the opening of higher education to women, the establishments of educational institutions for workingmen, and the rebirth of the spirit of learning in public schools and universities tended to break down the barriers between classes and to bridge

> chasms between minds. Educational processes quietly radiated, creating an intellectual climate which vastly favoured creative attitudes towards renovating the national order. Victorian education became England's alternative to success corps d'etat manifested by some other European nations.[28]

The conflict arises when the ideals of art and literature fall and seek inspiration not from real life and situations, but from mere fun and amusement and cheap materialistic pleasures. Having the aim to educate through art and literature, Shaw's drama gained the status of the Drama of Purpose. A critic will find the same trait in one of Shaw's important plays. According to Shaw:

> It (Pygmalion) is so intensely and deliberately didactic, and its subject is esteemed so dry, that I delight in throwing it at the heads of the wiseacres who repeat the parrot cry that the art should never be didactic. It goes to prove my contention that great art can never be anything else.[29]

It is indeed essential that the artist visualizes the larger purpose of art and creation, besides having a coherent and comprehensive view of human nature and life, in order to captivate the ultimate reality behind the world of senses and appearances with its relevance. Through Life Force, as coined and popularized by Shaw, the essence of life and spirit can be realized through the power of thought and understanding of the meaning behind creation of living worlds. This theory of Life Force is the most dominating evolutionary mark underlying Shaw's plays. *Man and Superman* remains witness to this theory in support, culminating on even a larger theory of Creative Evolution in *Back to Methuselah*. Through the prized gift of intellect and the faculty of mind and thought, together with the will to attain imagination and desire lead to creation. Shaw further explains this process through dramatizing situations from the earliest time of Adam and Eve, crossing barriers of time and epochs, combining extraordinary experiences till the time as far as thought can reach. In his series of plays in *Back to Methuselah*, we find man's continued effort to pursue further, besides his destiny, and nature playing its part through Life Force. This Life Force does not have man as its only agent but equally or the more active participant here is women.

Shaw has quite naturally defined the position of these two most important agents, man and woman behind the functioning of civilization from precedent to precedent. In this way, we can see a noiseless revolution for women upliftment, righty based upon in securing her actual position the nature has bestowed. But the theory of Life Force needs extension. Human life and its related progress are thus, in a ceaseless stream, crossing over the boundaries of gender, creed, class, caste and colour. It levels human experiences through the time bar. Shaw places himself in the process where he as an artist is also caught by nature to perform the task for mankind in general. Shaw writes in the Postscript of *Back to Methuselah*:

> An author is an instrument in the grip of Creative Evolution, and may find himself starting a movement to which in his own little person he is intensely opposed. When I am writing a play I never invent a plot: I let the play write itself and shape itself, which it always does even when up to the last moment I do not forsee the way out. Sometimes I do...I do not see what the play was driving at until quite a long time after I have finished it; and even then I may be wrong about it just as any critical third party may.[30]

Thus, man alone of all the creations can help the process of Creative Evolution. Human life and its related progress subsist in the context of Life Force, moving in ceaseless stream crossing over the boundaries of death in the shape of resurrection.

At the very same time, we find Shaw apprehensive of the historical progress made by mankind, but he remembers that "Evolution keeps creeping in."[31] In fact, he is critical of the superiority complex his own generation is suffering from, with the false notion of progress of having outrun the past, calling the medieval and other epochs as Dark Ages. He is sure that such nasty pronouncements and stupid claims, just account for the sheer ignorance of people in being convinced of their little achievements as a height of civilization and philosophy. Shaw quite reasonably rejects Macaulay's faith in progress. Zoo argues with The Elderly Gentleman in *Back to Methuselah* highlighting the required awareness for better living. She says, "It is not the number of years we have behind us, but the number we have before us, that makes us careful and responsible and determined to find out the truth about everything."[32] Shaw's works seem to be the embodiment of his anti-Victorian bent. He is no doubt deeply committed to the idea that there has been no progress in history so far but he has an equally deep commitment to the possibility of progress in the future. In this crucial scenario, if our civilization is facing crises where tremendous human capacity is called for, then of course mankind will have to rise to face the challenges and achieve such heights and this is exactly the same scenario Shaw presents in his *Back to Methuselah*. He holds on to the optimistic side of things having a firm belief in paradoxes of life; the dual theory of decline and progress. For Macaulay, Victorian England is the glorious period in the history of mankind and its highest achievement, but for Shaw, mankind and the masses, and its making of the Superman is nature's highest achievement so far. Shaw asserts:

> I, as a Creative Evolutionist, postulate a creative Life Force or Evolutionary Appetite seeking power over circumstances and mental development by the method of Trial and Error, making mistake after mistake, but still winning its finally irresistible way.[33]

There comes a time when "a man needs to meditate in solitude on his destiny."[34] This destiny is again a design of life that can be achieved if man tries to explore the nature of things around. In the contemporary setting, the dramatist could find apparent progress that money made, but it is disillusioning to find any concrete reform in characters of people and statesmanship of nation in the process involved. It is indeed the modification in human character that could create the possibility of progress in morality, religion and politics. Shaw's powerful medium of expression is his drama, and this can hardly be cut down to the mediocre level of mere fun and amusement. It is a sure means to solve the serious and urgent emerging issues and problems of society with appropriate solutions, and "try to open my reader's eye to the political facts under which they live. I cannot change their minds; but I can increase their knowledge,"[35] reflects Shaw.

These are the ideas and the message G.B. Shaw had to transmit through his brilliant evolutionary dramatic presentations. Having been able to exploit the opportunity of sharing the last and the first halves of the nineteenth and the twentieth century respectively, he could, indeed, consider both Victorian and Modern eras as his contemporary background for his works with the firm resolve to bring change and reform in the domain of drama. Unlike Ibsen and other cotemporary playwrights, he could provide possible solutions to the problems. It cannot be enough to expose what is hidden and what is not pleasant, but an effort to give solutions for turning unpleasant to pleasant can be a remarkable challenge for a sincere artist. Shaw's works run parallel to this concept adhering to it religiously. He never leaves anything unsolved, though his debates and arguments may be lengthy but they always are interesting and end with some proper solution to fit into the sphere of human acceptance. Surely, they tend to shock us sometimes.

Indeed art and literature, sans a message of life, by interpreting and solving their associated issues, in the context of fluctuating human needs and aspirations, would be of little worth and would soon dwindle away like the "brief candle" or "the walking shadow". The work and evaluation of such an art or dramatic art like Shaw's can be better appreciated and realized when compared and contrasted not only with the contemporary art and artists, but also with those who have preceded him. Among Shaw's great predecessors the overall most towering personality is that of Shakespeare, the poet dramatist. When we think of Shakespeare, we cannot but think of the man as a brilliant product and representative of Renaissance. His poetic drama is remarkably evident of the fundamentals of Renaissance the base of which is the love of the romantic, or romance; the search for the beautiful and passion for the wonderful. In fact, Shakespeare's dramatic art is nothing if not romantic, covering long and brilliant list of his tragedies, tragic-comedies, comedies, and historic plays. A very interesting and useful contrast with G.B. Shaw here could be that, basically, while, Shakespeare is a romantic poet dramatist, Shaw declaredly is anti-romantic and rationalist prose dramatist. Yet they both have some meeting ground, in the sense that they are both creative dramatists, with profound insight into human nature. Both borrowed their ideas and techniques to some extent from near and remote sources and later improved and enriched them into products of their own: Shakespeare from the plots of the University Wits, Shaw took his ideas from Henrik Ibsen. Both have influenced the world of literature and left a mark, becoming legend and part of history. But perhaps the similarities end here, and we begin analyzing the points of distinction between them. Shakespeare was both a great entertainer and painter of subtle and profound human feelings, covering the intricacies inherited by man along with the diverse situations and remained keenest and the sharpest of the observers of those intricacies. His dramas are remarkable illustrations of his incredible imaginative and reflective quality unmatched in perhaps in the entire world literature. We not only admire and enjoy his dramatic pieces but become part of his dramatic personae. Though apparently not didactic, Shakespeare's ideas, his plots and his characters and characterization breathe fresh lives into our blood and bones. On the other hand, Shaw, following the dramatic trend of Drama of Idea and Purpose, developed his plays on evolutionary and didactic pattern. Nonetheless, Shaw with all his sermonizing and message giving, along with his passion for diagnosing and analyzing things, and most importantly apart from offering solution to whatever needs to be resolved, remains creative and evolutionary. Like Shakespeare whose drama underwent a distinct process of evolution in respect of maturity in both idea and technique, Shaw wrote his plays on the same pattern of evolution. A comparative estimate of the two great playwrights, indeed, highlights Shaw's dramatic genius in the light of what he did in his own drama which Shakespeare could do in his own. The attempt here is not to determine the superiority of the one over the other; it is but to find out if with all his versatility, and universalism in respect of philosophy and art, Shaw succeeds in his mission of "changing the Nation" to "my opinion", coupled with his evolutionary effort of turning the old dramatic legacies of Comedy of Manners into Drama of Ideas and Purpose. True, Shaw is nothing if not revolutionary, he is all the time anxious enough to "blow off the borrowed earth and the heavens," with the mission of building upon "the ashes of it a world of his own."[36] Goethe, the celebrated German poet and philosopher coined for the great prophets of old, the unique and forceful terminology of the "living wave", which remains busy in gathering streams and rivers into the endless ocean. Perhaps the same could be said of Shaw through whose remarkable dramatic efforts, the legacies of art and ideas reached its summit.

Shaw's dramatic prose is meant to suit the temper of his own drama, the Drama of Ideas, written to correct and reform existing institutions through analysis and evaluation which is meant not only to dramatize or entertain. Free from the savagery of Swift and the sadistic vain of Dryden, Shaw is a satirist with a missionary zeal to reform. In his satiric way, there is nothing like despair or pessimism about his art and ideas. Great satirists are evidently critics whose target is to correct human and social vices and follies. The aim is to laugh at the follies and weaknesses out of countenance. A satirist is mostly bitter, savage, and sharp and even maybe brutal, while the humorist is free of any strains of bitterness. The illustrious literary critic and historian, Cazamian, suggests that satire is the leading feature of Shaw's plays and laughter is merely the sugar coating applied over the bitter pills. There is of course always ceaseless undercurrent of satire running through his dramatic works, ridiculing and exposing the existing courts and conventions. It warns about the hypocrisy. Shaw is busy attacking and pulling down old idols, exuberating their faults, but all on a purpose, which is to mend and reform. His stroke spares no institution or department of thought and action. The conventional concept of family and marriage, love and romance, war and religion, the cult of shallow respectability and superficial democracy, all come under his lash but with a view to reconstruct and renew life. In all his works, he can be distinguished from the general satirist, maintaining his poise and balance of grace and higher purpose. As observed, Shaw instead of starting from the presumptions of the evil in man thrives on the essential goodness of man which under the nourishing nectar of his philosophy of Life Force is all ascending with the gradual radiance of a superior personal race. It serves to impart a benevolence not always recognized, but invariably present, which makes him an artist unique and loveable. Marked by satiric venture, his plays aspire for a fresh new world, to be organized and managed by some superior race and the arrival of Superman. All his comments and critical pronouncements regarding institutions follow the same spirit of correction and reform. It is his firm belief that there is always scope for improvement and movement towards evolution. If we think fairly, deeply and realistically over the issues, mere mechanical discoveries and inventions may not mark and signify genuine progress and admiration for modern civilization. According to Shaw, progress cannot be identified with "steam engine and electric telegraph." True progress calls for excellence in the quality of human character and personality, its intellect and moral values. Elsewhere, targeting the West in general and Britain in particular, Shaw puts them to account for turning our planet into a hub of trade and merchandise. He warns them that all their achievements will soon come to naught. It is never an increased command over the world of matter, but rather a desire and will to bring about improvement in human faculties of thought and action. As for today, our material lives may have been improvised over the last centuries, but we continue to despair with the threat of nuclear war, apart from the rempant violence, terror, poverty and penury, and tarnishing of humanitarian values.

For Shaw it is not definitely the art alone that he is interested in, rather it is the message and the idea that he cares for. He is in favour of art for the sake of life, rather than art itself. What worth is the poet's eloquence or the musician's pipe or the moving breeze without a message? Shaw's Drama of Idea and Purpose, therefore, emphasizes the challenges and demands of life seeking solution in order to cope with the problem of culture and civilization.

There has been a paradigm shift in literature with changing time and taste of people. Shaw's work can be seen in continuation with human experiences. It homogenises and accumulates this valuable experience of life. His art is connected to the rudiments of human nature that ultimately serves humanity at large. The novelty of his dramatic art lies in its being solely for a purpose. His art and ideas, theories and philosophies all stand committed to life and its institutions. It is indeed, in the nature of things that our life and the life around us, from time to time, should call for sessions of rebirth and renewal of its faculties and organizations, to help and share in the forward move of its Creative Evolution under the Wise, forceful and benign command of Life Force. The strains of our art and literature, our ideas and philosophies, however, those tremendous and blissful tools of elucidating this divine creative process, slows down or sometimes dries up for want of the right supply of the required vision along with resolve on the part of the artist. It is so because the great and invaluable art, according to its mode and spirit of service as well as survival has always been subject to some higher promise and commitments of prophetic proportions. Such demands and challenges were met in the past only by men of colossal courage and conviction and fortunately enough near to our own times by G.B. Shaw, who has been one of the much maligned, debased, greatly debated and most controversial of literary figures in history. He is the one who struck a note of warning by marking a definite break in the realm of Western art of drama and philosophy, through his eloquent declaration of rebellion and war against the mentally destitute, socially, morally, spiritually and aesthetically decadent messy trash, donning the cloak of art and artistic trends, shocking the West with visible cracks and undeniable tremors in its structure. It is this stand that keeps him apart and distinguished from millions of other artists and dramatists in the world of literature. Nearly, a century has elapsed and we continue to find Shaw's art and ideas in perennial vogue, crossing the barriers of culture, caste, colour, creed, and nationalities in our present post-modern globalized context. Nonetheless, this tireless spirit of reform and reconstruction in human institutions, gave a message of delivering art and philosophy from the shackles of theatrical fun and buffoonery. Shaw's art is founded on a dynamic and pulsating creative urge, inspired by a profound sense of history, compassing the essential goodness of man and an invariable possibility of hope, love and charity for a better world, human prospects, and promise of holding and preserving the divine trust, echoing Browning's melodious assurance and promise:

> Grow old along with me!
> The best is yet to be...[37]

Notes

1. Shaw. "Back to Methuselah." ed. Dan H.L. *The Bodely Head Bernard Shaw Collected Plays with their Prefaces*. Vol. 5. London: Max Reinhardt, 1972. p. 430.
2. *Ibid.*
3. Shaw. "Epistle Dedicatory." *Man and Superman*. ed. Dan H.L. *The Bodely Head Bernard Shaw Collected Plays with their Prefaces*. Vol. 2. London: Max Reinhardt, 1980. p. 527.
4. Shaw. "Preface." *The Devil's Disciple*. ed. Dan H.L. *The Bodely Head Bernard Shaw Collected Plays with their Prefaces*. Vol. 2. London: Max Reinhardt, 1980. p. 44.
5. *Ibid.*, p. 45.
6. Shaw. "Man and Superman." ed. Dan H.L. *The Bodely Head Bernard Shaw Collected Plays with their Prefaces*. Vol. 2. London: Max Reinhardt, 1980. p. 534.
7. *Ibid.*, p. 535.
8. Shaw. "The Devil's Disciple." ed. Dan H.L. *The Bodely Head Bernard Shaw Collected Plays with their Prefaces*. Vol. 2. London: Max Reinhardt, 1980. p. 30.
9. Shaw. *Caesar and Cleopatra*. "The New Statesman." London, 3 May 1913. p. 311.
10. Shaw. "Preface." *The Devil's Disciple*. ed. Dan H.L. *The Bodely Head Bernard Shaw Collected Plays with their Prefaces*. Vol. 2. London: Max Reinhardt, 1980. p. 29.
11. Shaw. *Caesar and Cleopatra by the Author of the Play*. "The New Statesman." London, 3 May 1913. ed. Dan H.L. *The Bodely Head Bernard Shaw Collected Plays with their Prefaces*. Vol. 2. London: Max Reinhardt, 1980. p. 310.
12. *Ibid.*, p. 321.
13. *Ibid.*
14. Shaw. "Man and Superman." ed. Dan H.L. *The Bodely Head Bernard Shaw Collected Plays with their Prefaces*. Vol. 2. London: Max Reinhardt, 1980. p. 515.
15. "Bernard Shaw Talks about Actors and Acting." *Shaw on Theatre*. ed. E.J. West. New York: Hill and Wang, 1959. p. 198.
16. Shaw. "Epistle Dedicatory." *Man and Superman*. ed. Dan H.L. *The Bodely Head Bernard Shaw Collected Plays with their Prefaces*. Vol. 2. London: Max Reinhardt, 1980. p. 527.
17. *Ibid.*

18. H. Arthur Jones. "American Drama is Suffering from an Overdose of IDEAS." *The New York Times*. 12 July 1914.
19. Shaw. "Epistle Dedicatory." *Man and Superman*. ed. Dan H.L. *The Bodely Head Bernard Shaw Collected Plays with their Prefaces*. Vol. 2. London: Max Reinhardt, 1980. p. 509.
20. Shaw. "Misalliance." ed. Dan H.L. *The Bodely Head Bernard Shaw Collected Plays with their Prefaces*. Vol. 4. London: Max Reinhardt, 1972. p. 466.
21. Shaw. Misalliance. An interview drafted by Shaw. "The Drama of THE TWENTY-FIRST CENTURY." *The Observer*. 12 June 1910. ed. Dan H.L. *The Bodely Head Bernard Shaw Collected Plays with their Prefaces*. Vol. 4. London: Max Reinhardt, 1972. p. 262.
22. Shaw. "John Bull's Other Island." ed. Dan H.L. *The Bodely Head Bernard Shaw Collected Plays with their Prefaces*. Vol. 2. London: Max Reinhardt, 1980. p. 814.
23. Shaw. "Misalliance." ed. Dan H.L. *The Bodely Head Bernard Shaw Collected Plays with their Prefaces*. Vol. 4. London: Max Reinhardt, 1972. p. 138.
24. J.L. Wisenthal. *Shaw's Sense of History*. Oxford: Clarendon, 1988. p. vii.
25. A.L. Rowse. "The Use of History." *The Reinterpretation of Victorian Literature*. ed. Joseph E. Baker. New Jersey: Princeton University, 1950. p. 18.
26. J.L. Wisenthal. *Shaw's Sense of History*. Oxford: Clarendon, 1988. p. 78.
27. Shaw. Caesar and Cleopatra by the Author of the Play. "The New Statesman." London, 3 May 1913. ed. Dan H.L. *The Bodely Head Bernard Shaw Collected Plays with their Prefaces*. Vol. 2. London: Max Reinhardt, 1980. p. 314.
28. William S. Knickerbocker. "Victorian Education and the Idea of Culture." *The Reinterpretation of Victorian Literature*. ed. Joseph E. Baker. New Jersey: Princeton University, 1950. p. 97.
29. Shaw. "Pygmalion." ed. Dan H.L. *The Bodely Head Bernard Shaw Collected Plays with their Prefaces*. Vol. 4. London: Max Reinhardt, 1972. p. 663.
30. Shaw. "Postscript: After Twenty Five Years." *Back to Methuselah*. ed. Dan H.L. *The Bodely Head Bernard Shaw Collected Plays with their Prefaces*. Vol. 5. London: Max Reinhardt, 1972. p. 685.
31. *Ibid*., p. 691.
32. Shaw. "Back to Methuselah." ed. Dan H.L. *The Bodely Head Bernard Shaw Collected Plays with their Prefaces*. Vol. 5. London: Max Reinhardt, 1972. p. 516.

33. Shaw. "Preface." *Far Fetched Fables*. ed. Dan H.L. *The Bodely Head Bernard Shaw Collected Plays with their Prefaces*. Vol. 7. London: Max Reinhardt, 1974. p. 396.
34. Shaw. "Misalliance." ed. Dan H.L. *The Bodely Head Bernard Shaw Collected Plays with their Prefaces*. Vol. 4. London: Max Reinhardt, 1972. p. 173.
35. Shaw. "Preface to Geneva." ed. Dan H.L. *The Bodely Head Bernard Shaw Collected Plays with their Prefaces*. Vol. 7. London: Max Reinhardt, 1974. p. 30.
36. Mohammad Iqbal. *Kulliate-Iqbal*. Delhi: Kutub Khana Azizia, 2002.
37. Robert Browning. "Rabbi Ben Ezra." *The Oxford Book of English Mystical Verse*. ed. Nicholson and Lee. Oxford: the Clarendon Press, 1917.

Bibliography

Primary Sources

Shaw, George Bernard. *The Bodely Head Bernard Shaw Collected Plays with their Prefaces*. Ed. Dan H. Lawrence. 7 Vols. London: Hamilton, 1974.

______. *Major Critical Essays*. Middlesex: Penguin, 1986.

______. *Preface Bernard Shaw*. London: Hamilton, 1965.

______. *Everybody's Political What's What*. London: n.p., 1944.

______. *The Intelligent Woman's Guide to Socialism and Capitalism*. New York: Bretano's, 1928.

______. *The Religious Speeches of Bernard Shaw*. ed. Warren Sylvester Smith, Pennsylvania State University, 1963.

______. *Selected Non-Dramatic Writings of Bernard Shaw*. ed. Dan H. Lawrence. Cambridge, Mass. Riverside: Houghton Miffilin, 1965.

______. "Bernard Shaw Talks about Actors and Acting", *Shaw on Theatre*. ed. E.J. West. New York: Hill and Wang, 1959.

______. *Our Theatre in the Nineties*. ed. Hunekar. London: George Allan and Unwin, 1932.

______. "Misalliance, An interview drafted by Shaw, The Drama of THE TWENTY-FIRST CENTURY." *The Observer*. 12 June 1910.

______. *Quintessence of Ibsenism*. London: Constable, 1932.

______. *An Unsocial Socialist*. London: Swan Sonnenschein, Lowry & Co., 1887.

______. *The Black Girl in Search of God and Some Lesser Tales.* London: Constable, 1934.

______. *Who I am, and What I Think: Sixteen Self Sketches.* London: Constable, 1949.

______. *The Matter with Ireland.* London: Hart-Davis, 1962.

Secondary Sources/Books

Armstrong, C.F. *Shakespeare to Shaw.* London: Mills and Boon, 1913.

Barker, Granvill. *On Dramatic Method.* New York: Hill and Wang, 1964.

Bentley, Eric. *Bernard Shaw.* New York: Applause Books, 2002.

______. *The Playwright as Thinker.* New York: The World, 1964.

Bloom, Harold. *George Bernard Shaw.* Broomall, Pa.: Chelsea House, 2000.

Bradbrook, M.C. *Ibsen the Norwegian: A Revaluation.* London: Chanto and Windus, 1946.

Brecht, B. *Brecht on Theatre*, 1964.

Brown, I. *Shaw and His Time.* London: Greenwood, 1979.

Cazamian, L. *A History of English Literature.* Madras: Macmillan, 1985.

Cesterton, *G.K. George Bernard Shaw.* UK: Echo Library, 2008.

Collins, *G.B. Shaw.* London: Jonathan Cape, 1925.

Colbourn, Maurice. *The Real Bernard Shaw.* London: n.p., 1949.

Cole, Toby. *Playwright on Playwrights.* New York: Hill and Wang, 1964.

Crouch, A.P. *Mr. G.B. Shaw.* New York: Norwood Editions, 1975.

Daiches, D. *A Critical History of English Literature.* Vol. 4, New Delhi: Allied, 1983.

Duffin, H.C. *Quintessence of Bernard Shaw.* Delhi: Doaba House, 1998.

Dutta, K.N. *G.B.S. The Potter and the Wheel: A Revelation.* London: n.p., 1920.

Dutta, Rajini Palme. *George Bernard Shaw: A Memoir*. New York: Folcroft Library Edition, 1977.

Eliot, T.S. *Poetry and Drama*. London: Faber and Faber, 1951.

Evans, B. Ifor. *A Short History of English Literature*. Harmonsworth: Penguine, 1961.

Fjelde, Rolf. (Ed.) *Ibsen: A Collection of Critical Essays*. London: Prentice-Hall Cliffs, 1966.

Former, E.U. *The Irish Dramatic Movement*. London: Methuen, 1954.

Gerene, Nicholas. *Bernard Shaw: A Critical View*. London: Palgrave Macmillan, 1987.

Gibbs, A.M. *Art and Mind of Shaw*. London: Macmillan, 1953.

Handerson, A. *G.B. Shaw: Man of the Century*. New York: D. Appleton, 1932.

Holroyd, M. *The Genius of Shaw: A Symposium*. London: Hodder and Stoughten, 1979.

_______. *Bernard Shaw*. New York: Random House, 1982.

Huang, J. *Shaw and Galsworthy*. London: O.U.P., 1979.

Hudson, W.H. *An Outline History of English Literature*. Delhi: A.I.T.B.S., 2007.

Hugo, K. *Bernard Shaw: Playwright and Preacher*. London: Methuen, 1971.

Ibsen, Henrik. *A Doll's House*. Trans. W. Arther. Chennai: Macmillan, 1997.

_____. *Ghost and Other Plays*. Trans. P. Watts. New York: Penguine Books, 1985.

_____. *Selected Plays by Ibsen*. Trans. W. Archer. New York: Penguine Books, 1962.

Iqbal, Mohammad. "Bale-Jibraeel." *Kulliyate-Iqbal*. Delhi: Kutub Khana Azizia, 2002.

Jahan, R. *The Ibsen-Shaw Kinship*. Calcutta: Writers Workshop, 2002.

Joad, C.E.M. *Shaw and Society*. London: Odhams Press, 1951.

Kalidasa. *Abhijnana Sakuntalam: A Critical Study, Sharad Ramjiwale*. Delhi: Rama Brothers, 2006.

Kaufmann, R.J. *G.B. Shaw: A Collection of Critical Essays*. New Jersey: Prentice Hall, 1965.

Khayyam, Omar. *Rubaiyat. Palgrave's Golden Treasury*. Trans. Fitzgerald. Calcutta: Oxford University, 1997.

Knickerbocker, William S et al. *The Reinterpretation of Victorian Literature*, "Victorian Education and the Idea of Culture". Ed. Joseph E. Barker. New Jersey: Princeton University, 1950.

Knight, G. Wilson. *The Wheel of Fire: Interpretation of Shakespearian Tragedy*, 4th ed. London: Methuen, 1949.

_____. *The Golden Labyrinth*. New York: N. Norton, 1962.

Krutch, J. 'Modernism' in *Modern Drama*. New York: Cornel University, 1953.

Leavis, F.R. *The Common Pursuit*. London: Penguin, 1964.

Lumby, Y. *Trends in Twentieth Century Drama*. London: O.U.P., 1956.

MacFarlane, *J.W. Ibsen and Temper of Norwegian Literature*. London: O.U.P., 1960.

Marlow, Christopher. *Dr. Faustus*. United States: Kessinger. 2004.

Meisel, Martin. *Shaw and the Nineteenth Century Theatre*. New Jersey: Princeton University, 1963.

Morgan, Walter. *Why I like Bernard Shaw*. London: O.U.P., 1976.

Nicoll, Allardyce. *British Drama*. 5th ed. Delhi: Doaba House, 2005.

Northam, John. *Ibsen's Dramatic Method*. London: Faber and Faber, 1953.

Ohman, R.N. *Shaw: The Style and the Man*. Middleton: Wesleyans University, 1962.

Pearson, H. *Bernard Shaw: His Life and Personality*. London: Methuen, 1962.

Peters, Sally. *Bernard Shaw: The Ascent of the Superman*. New Haven: Yale University, 1996.

Russell, Bertrand. *History of Western Philosophy*. London: Unwin Brothers, 1954.

Pope, Alexander. *An Essay on Criticism*. London: n.p., 1711.

Reynolds, D. *Modern Drama*. London: Methuen, 1949.

Ricket, R.C. *History of English Literature*. New Delhi: U.B.S., 1995.

Roberts, R.E. *Henrik Ibsen: Critical Study*. London: Martic Socker, 1912.

Sengupta, S.C. *The Art of Bernard Shaw*. Calcutta: A. Mukherjee, 1960.

Shakespeare, William. *As You Like It*, Ed. Vinita Chandra. Delhi: Worldview, 2000.

_____. *The Complete Works of Shakespeare*. New York: Nelson Doubleday, 1946.

Shelley, P.B. *Ode to West Wind and Other Poems*. New York: Dover, 1993.

Smart, John. *Contexts in Literature: Twentieth Century British Drama*. Cambridge: Cambridge University, 2001.

Strindberg, August. *Miss Julie*. Trans. Helen Cooper. London: Methuen, 2000.

Tennyson, Alfred. *Morte D'Arthur*. Delhi: Aarti Book, 2004.

Trivedi, R.D. *A Compendious History of English Literature*. New Delhi: Vikas, 1978.

Ward, A.C. *Twentieth Century English Literature*. Madras: Macmillan, 1985.

Watson, B.B. *A Shavian Guide*. London: Chanto and Windus, 1964.

Williamson, A. *Theatre of Two Decades*. London: Cambridge University, 1951.

Williams, R. *Drama from Ibsen to Eliot*. London: Penguin Books, 1964.

Winsten, Stephen. *Days with Bernard Shaw*. London: Reader's Union, Hutchinson, 1951.

Wisenthal, J.L. *Shaw's Sense of History*. Oxford: Clarendon, 1988.

Articles and Essays

Auden, W.H. "The Fabian Figures". *Commonweal*. London, 23 October 1942.

Berlin, Normand. "Traffic of Our Stage: Why Waiting for Godot?" *The Massachusetts Review*. Amherst. Autumn, 1999.

Carlyle, Thomas. "Sir Walter Scott". *Critical and Miscellaneous Essays*. iv 33 works.

Freeman, John. "G.B.S." *The Moderns*. London, 1916.

Huneker, James. "Quintessence of Bernard Shaw". *Iconclasts*. New York, 1906.

Jain, Madhu. *India Today*. 15 October 1994.

Jones, Henry A. "American Drama is Suffering from Overdose of Ideas". *New York Times*. 12 July 1914.

Nair, Anita. "Mahesh Dattani—The Invisible Observer". 8 December 2009.

Tynan, Kenneth. *The Observer*, 1993.